RECENT RESEARCHES IN THE MUSIC OF THE MIDDLE AGES AND EARLY RENAISSANCE, 39

Johannes Martini and Johannes Brebis

Sacred Music

Part 1
Hymns, Magnificats, Motets, and Passions

Edited by Murray Steib

A-R Editions, Inc.
Middleton, Wisconsin

A-R Editions, Inc., Middleton, Wisconsin
© 2009 by A-R Editions, Inc.

All rights reserved. No part of this book may be reproduced or transmitted in any form by any electronic or mechanical means (including photocopying, recording, or information storage and retrieval) without permission in writing from the publisher.

The purchase of this edition does not convey the right to perform it in public, nor to make a recording of it for any purpose. Such permission must be obtained in advance from the publisher.

A-R Editions is pleased to support scholars and performers in their use of *Recent Researches* material for study or performance. Subscribers to any of the *Recent Researches* series, as well as patrons of subscribing institutions, are invited to apply for information about our "Copyright Sharing Policy."

The primary source for Martini's Magnificat 3. toni [1], Magnificat 4. toni, and Magnificat 6. toni is Vatican City, Biblioteca Apostolica Vaticana, MS Cappella Sistina 15, © 2009 Biblioteca Apostolica Vaticana. The musical text for nos. 14, 16, and 17 in this edition may not be performed or republished without the written approval of the Biblioteca Apostolica Vaticana.

Printed in the United States of America

ISBN-13: 978-0-89579-648-6
ISBN-10: 0-89579-648-1
ISSN: 0362-3572

♾ The paper used in this publication meets the minimum requirements of the American National Standard for Information Sciences—Permanence of Paper for Printed Library Materials, ANSI Z39.48-1992.

Contents

Abbreviations and Sigla vii

Acknowledgments ix

Introduction xi

  The Composers xi
  The Anonymous Psalm Settings xi
  The Hymns xii
  The Magnificats xiii
  The Other Motets xiii
  The "Salve Regina" Problem xv
  Evaluation of the Sources xv
  Notes on Performance xvii
  Notes xvii

Critical Commentary xix

  Editorial Methods xix
  Critical Notes xxi
  Notes xxxix

Plates xl

Hymns, Magnificats, Motets, and Passions
  (All works are probably by Martini unless otherwise indicated.)

Hymns

  1. Audi, benigne conditor 3
  2. Aures ad nostras *(odd-numbered stanzas by Brebis, even-numbered stanzas by Martini)* 5
  3. Ave maris stella 8
  4. Deus tuorum militum (1) *(odd-numbered stanzas by Brebis, even-numbered stanzas by Martini)* 10
  5. Deus tuorum militum (2) 13
  6. Exultet celum laudibus 16
  7. Festum nunc celebre 19
  8. Iste confessor 22
  9. Jesu, corona virginum 23
  10. Sanctorum meritis *(odd-numbered stanzas by Brebis, even-numbered stanzas by Martini)* 25
  11. Tibi, Christe, splendor 28
  12. Vexilla regis *(odd-numbered stanzas by Brebis, even-numbered stanzas by Martini)* 30

Magnificats

13. Magnificat 1. toni   33
14. Magnificat 3. toni (1)   36
15. Magnificat 3. toni (2)   43
16. Magnificat 4. toni   54
17. Magnificat 6. toni   73
18. Magnificat 6. toni, *Johannes Brebis*   94
19. Magnificat 8. toni (1)   100
20. Magnificat 8. toni (2)   102
21. Magnificat 8. toni (3)   109

Motets Based on Liturgical Texts

22. Ave decus virginale *(Sequence)*   112
23. Da pacem, Domine *(Benediction for Peace)*   115
24. Domine, non secundum *(Tract)*   118
25. Levate capita vestra *(Christmas Antiphons)*   124
26. O beate Sebastiane   135

Passions

27. Jesum Nazarenum *(St. John Passion)*   142
28. Non in die festo *(St. Matthew Passion)*   147

Celebretory Motets

29. Perfunde celi rore   161
30. Hercules omni memorandus evo, *Johannes Brebis*   170

Motet of Doubtful Attribution

31. Salve Regina   185

Abbreviations and Sigla

Manuscript Sources

BarcBC 454	Barcelona. Biblioteca de Catalunya. M.454.
DresSL 1/D/505	Dresden. Sächsische Landesbibliothek. MS Mus. 1/D/505 (*olim* Annaberg. Bibliothek der St. Annenkirche. MS 1248).
MilD 1	Milan. Archivio della Veneranda Fabbrica del Duomo, Sezione musicale. Librone 1 (*olim* 2269).
ModE M.1.11	Modena. Biblioteca Estense e Universitaria. MS α.M.1.11 (Lat. 454; *olim* V.H.11).
ModE M.1.12	Modena. Biblioteca Estense e Universitaria. MS α.M.1.12 (Lat. 455; *olim* V.H.9).
ModE X.1.11	Modena. Biblioteca Estense e Universitaria. MS α.X.1.11 (Lat. 471; *olim* VI.H.15).
MunBS 3154	Munich. Bayerische Staatsbibliothek, Musiksammlung. Musica MS 3154 ("Chorbuch des Nikolaus Leopold").
TrentC 91	Trent. Castello del Buonconsiglio. Monumenti e collezioni provinciali (ex Museo Provinciale d'Arte). MS 91.
VatS 15	Vatican City. Biblioteca Apostolica Vaticana. MS Cappella Sistina 15.
VatS 35	Vatican City. Biblioteca Apostolica Vaticana. MS Cappella Sistina 35.
VerBC 758	Verona. Biblioteca Capitolare. MS DCCLVIII.
VerBC 759	Verona. Biblioteca Capitolare. MS DCCLIX.

Printed Sources

1503[1]	Petrucci, Ottaviano. *Motetti De Passione, De Cruce, De Sacramento, De Beata Virgine Et Huiusmodi B*. Venice, 1503.
1505[2]	Petrucci, Ottaviano. *Motetti libro quarto*. Venice, 1505.

Reference Materials and Modern Editions

AH	*Analecta hymnica medii aevi*. Edited by Clemens Blume and Guido M. Dreves. 55 vols. Leipzig: O. R. Reisland, 1886–1922. Reprint, New York: Johnson Reprint Corporation, 1961.
AMMM	*Archivium Musices Metropolitanum Mediolanense*. Edited by Luciano Migliavacca et al. 16 vols. Milan: Veneranda Fabbrica del Duomo, 1958–69.

Brawley	Brawley, John Gray. "The Magnificats, Hymns, Motets, and Secular Compositions of Johannes Martini." 2 vols. Ph.D. diss., Yale University, 1968.
DrakePM	Drake, George Warren James. "The First Printed Books of Motets, Petrucci's Motetti A Numero Trentatre A (Venice, 1502) and Motetti De Passione, De Cruce, De Sacramento, De Beata Virgine Et Huiusmodi B (Venice, 1503): A Critical Study and Complete Edition." Ph.D. diss., University of Illinois, 1972.
DrakeMRM	Drake, Warren, ed. *Motetti de Passione, de Cruce, de Sacramento, de Beata Virgine et Huiusmodi B.* Monuments of Renaissance Music, vol. 11. Chicago: University of Chicago Press, 2002.
Gerber	Martini, Johannes. *Drei geistliche Gesänge.* Edited by Rudolf Gerber. Das Chorwerk, vol. 46. Wolfenbüttel: Möseler, 1937.
KanazawaP	Kanazawa, Masakata. "Polyphonic Music for Vespers in the Fifteenth Century." Ph.D. diss., Harvard University, 1966.
Lerner	Lerner, Edward R. "The Polyphonic Magnificat in Fifteenth-Century Italy." *Musical Quarterly* 50 (1964): 44–58.
Lockwood	Lockwood, Lewis. *Music in Renaissance Ferrara, 1400–1505.* Cambridge: Harvard University Press, 1984.
LU	*The Liber Usualis.* Edited by the Benedictines of Solesmes. Various editions, including Tournai: Desclée & Co., 1963.
MGG	*Die Musik in Geschichte und Gegenwart; allgemeine Enzyklopädie der Musik.* Edited by Friedrich Blume. Kassel, Bärenreiter-Verlag, 1949–79.
Noblitt	Noblitt, Thomas L., ed. *Der Kodex des Magister Nicolaus Leopold: Staatsbibliothek München Mus. ms. 3154.* Das Erbe deutscher Musik, vols. 80–83. Kassel: Bärenreiter, 1987–96.
Rifkin	Rifkin, Joshua. "Munich, Milan, and a Marian Motet: Dating Josquin's *Ave Maria . . . gratia plena.*" *Journal of the American Musicological Society* 56 (2003): 239–350.
Ros-Fábregas	Emilio Ros-Fábregas. "The Manuscript Barcelona, Biblioteca de Catalunya, M.454: Study and Edition in the Context of the Iberian and Continental Manuscript Traditions," 2 vols. Ph.D. diss., City University of New York, 1992.
Sherr	Sherr, Richard, ed. *Selections from Motetti libro quatro (Venice, 1505).* Sixteenth-Century Motet, vol. 3. New York: Garland, 1991.
Stephan	Stephan, Wolfgang. *Die burgundisch-nederländische Motette zur Zeit Ockeghems.* Kassel: Bärenreiter, 1937; reprint, 1973.
Walpole	Walpole, A. S. *Early Latin Hymns.* Cambridge: Cambridge University Press, 1922. Reprint, Hildesheim: Georg Olms, 1966.
Ward	Ward, Tom R. "The Polyphonic Office Hymn from the Late Fourteenth Century until the Early Sixteenth Century." Ph.D. diss., University of Pittsburgh, 1969.

Acknowledgments

One of the pleasures of completing a long-term project such as this is being able to thank the many people whose help and support not only made the work possible, but also made it much better than it otherwise might have been. First, I would like to thank Ball State University for a Summer Salary Award in 2003 that allowed me to work uninterrupted on the project in its early stages. I would also like to thank The Newberry Library, which awarded me the Lester J. Cappon Fellowship in Documentary Editing, also in 2003; everyone there was very helpful, especially Sara Austin, the Associate Director of Research and Education. Thomas Noblitt very kindly shared his personal microfilms with me and on several occasions clarified matters that were opaque to me. Joshua Rifkin kindly pointed out two anonymous hymns that he has attributed to Johannes Martini. Bonnie J. Blackburn and Leofranc Holford-Strevens helped with several of the Latin texts as well as liturgical and musical matters. Thomas Payne, Jeffrey Dean, and Michael McGrade also helped with the Latin. Numerous graduate and undergraduate assistants have helped me with various aspects of preparing the edition, and I would like to thank them all: Deborah Stark, Jace Wittig, Katie Coyle, Rosemary Keenan, and Megan Upchurch. My biggest single debt of gratitude goes to Stefano Mengozzi, who freely shared his expertise in Latin, editorial accidentals, and text underlay with me, and helped to make this a better edition overall.

I was very lucky to have two excellent performing groups sing several of Martini's motets. VivaVoce, conducted by Peter Schubert, performed one motet at the conference "Josquin and His Models: The Emergence of Pervasive Imitation" held at McGill University, 7–8 June 2003. The Ball State University Chamber Choir, conducted by Jeffrey Pappas, recorded part of a motet for me to use in a paper that I gave at the 40th Annual International Congress on Medieval Studies in Kalamazoo, 8 May 2005.

Introduction

The Composers

Very little is known about Johannes Martini before he began to work in Ferrara for Ercole I d'Este. The introduction to the edition of his complete masses contains a detailed biography, and very little new information has surfaced since then.[1] At that time, I said that Martini died between 21 October 1497, when Ercole mentions in a letter that he is gravely ill ("si gravimentè infermo"), and 29 December 1497, when Ercole refers to the vacancies in benefices caused by his death ("Inanti che vacassano li benefitij de Zoanne Martino nostro cantore per la morte sua").[2] We now know from a document from the Confraternita della Morte found by G. P. Calessi that Martini actually died on 23 October 1497: "Il 23 ottobre muore Zan Martin, cantore che avitava nella contrada di S. Croce e sepolto al Vescovado."[3]

As with Martini, very little is known about Johannes Brebis before he began to work in Ferrara for Ercole.[4] Like Martini, Brebis was among the first people that Ercole hired for his new cappella. The first document to mention Brebis dates from November 1471, where he is listed as "fra Zoane de Franza Cantadore." In 1478 Ercole appointed him to the post of archpriest of the parish church of Coccanile (less than fifteen miles from Ferrara), and he died shortly before 12 February 1479. Only six pieces are attributed to Brebis, making his known oeuvre quite small. ModE M.1.11–12 contains one Magnificat and the odd-numbered verses of four hymns: "Aures ad nostras," "Deus tuorum militum (1)," "Sanctorum meritis," and "Vexilla regis." All of these liturgical pieces were most likely composed at Ferrara for use in Ercole's court chapel. The only other known piece—"Hercules omni memorandus evo," a motet in honor of Ercole probably composed in 1472—is found in only one source, ModE X.1.11. In addition to these securely attributed works, Masakata Kanazawa has attributed one of the anonymous hymn sections in ModE M.1.11–12 to Brebis, and there is the possibility that he composed some portion of the remaining anonymous pieces in this manuscript.[5]

The Anonymous Psalm Settings

ModE M.1.11–12 contains sixty-nine anonymous settings of psalms and canticles, including thirty-five for daily vespers (five for each day of the week), and thirty-four for matins and lauds on Thursday, Friday, and Saturday of Holy Week (see table 1). It has long been argued that these psalm settings may have been written by Martini or Brebis, much like the hymns.[6] One of the most important reasons for this assertion is an entry in Modena, Archivio de Stato, Camera Ducale Estense, Guardaroba, 100, "Speso delo offitio del spect. Marco de Galeoto" from 1479: "Per uno libro de canto da Vespero per la capella de il prefato nostro Signore, composto da Giovan Martin compositore."[7] It is highly likely that this entry refers to the double-choir manuscript ModE M.1.11–12, and it would also explain why the only attributions to Martini that occur in the manuscript appear with the hymns that were co-written with Brebis.

The psalm settings are very simple pieces written for daily use in Ercole's chapel. They alternate verses between the two choirs, use a psalm tone in the top voice, and essentially move in homophonic parallel motion. Most of the settings are for two voices, and some of these are labeled "faulx bourdon," signifying performance with a third voice that is always a perfect fourth below the top voice; a few settings for three written-out voices are also found (e.g., "In exitu Israel"). Many, if not all, of the two-voice psalms that are not labeled "faulx bourdon" could be sung in this manner, but in this edition, I have only added the improvised voice where it is specified. Whoever wrote or compiled these pieces seems to have followed a few basic guidelines for the use of "faulx bourdon." None of the vesper settings call for this technique, and as only one of the thirty-five psalms uses three voices, it may be that these were meant to be sung in only two

TABLE 1
Arrangement of Psalms for Vespers, Matins, and
Lauds in ModE M.1.11–12

The Arrangement of the Daily Psalms for Vespers
   Feria prima (Sunday): Psalms 109, 110, 111, 112, 113
   Feria secunda (Monday): Psalms 114, 115, 116, 119, 120
   Feria tertia (Tuesday): Psalms 121, 122, 123, 124, 125
   Feria quarta (Wednesday): Psalms 126, 127, 128, 129, 130
   Feria quinta (Thursday): Psalms 131, 132, 134, 135, 136
   Feria sexta (Friday): Psalms 137, 138, 139, 140, 141
   Sabbato (Saturday): Psalms 143, 144, 145, 146, 147

The Arrangement of Holy Week Psalms and Canticles
   Feria quinta
     Matins
       Nocturn 1: Psalms 68, 69, 70
       Nocturn 2: Psalms 71, 72, 73
       Nocturn 3: Psalms 74, 75, 76
     Lauds
       Psalms 50, 89, 62/66
       Exodus 15:1–19
       Psalms 148–50
       Luke 1:68–79
   Feria sexta
     Matins
       Nocturn 1: Psalms 2, 21, 26
       Nocturn 2: Psalms 37, 39, 53
       Nocturn 3: Psalms 58, 87, 93
     Lauds
       Psalms 50, 142, 62/66
       Hebacuc 3:2–19
       Psalms 148–50
   Sabatto
     Matins
       Nocturn 1: Psalms 4, 14, 15
       Nocturn 2: Psalms 23, 26, 29
       Nocturn 3: Psalms 53, 75, 87
     Lauds
       Psalms 50, 42, 62/66
       Isaiah 38:10–20
       Psalm 89

voices. Furthermore, the term was never used in ModE M.1.12, but whether this meant that one side of the choir did not sing faulx bourdon or that the appearance of the term in ModE M.1.11 was meant to carry over to ModE M.1.12, we may never know.

The Hymns

Catholic services in Italy and Germany generally used different hymns for particular feasts; for example, on Sundays in Lent, services following the Italian tradition used the hymn "Aures ad nostras" whereas those following the German tradition used the hymn "Christe qui lux es et dies."[8] All but one of Martini's twelve extant hymn settings belong to the Italian tradition; the one exception is "Festum nunc celebre," the preferred hymn for Ascension in the German tradition. Not surprisingly, it exists uniquely in a German source: MunBS 3154 (see table 2). The majority of the hymns are three-voice settings that paraphrase the chant in the top voice and alternate verses between the two choirs; all of the exceptions ("Ave maris stella," "Deus tuorum militum [2]," "Festum nunc celebre," and "Tibi Christe splendor") are four-voice works written for a single choir. The double-choir hymns were almost certainly written specifically for Ercole's chapel and exist solely in ModE M.1.11–12; "Ave maris stella" and "Festum nunc celebre" were probably written before Martini arrived in Ferrara (neither exists in a Ferrarese source). Four of the double-choir hymns were composed by both Brebis and Martini, with Brebis composing the odd-numbered verses and Martini the even-numbered ones ("Aures ad nostras," "Deus tuorum militum [1]," "Sanctorum meritis," and "Vexilla regis"); some of the other four double-choir hymns also may have been written by both composers, but they either lack an ascription or are missing in ModE M.1.12; "Exultet celum laudibus," however, is by Martini alone. Joshua Rifkin has attributed the two anonymous four-voice hymns in ModE X.1.11 ("Deus tuorum militum [2]" and "Tibi Christe splendor") to Martini on the basis of the handwriting, and their style is indeed very similar to Martini's other hymns.[9] "Tibi Christe splendor" has the text to verses 2 and 4, suggesting that it was performed in alternatim: because no setting of the first and third verses exists in a Ferrarese source, it is quite possible that this setting was sung in alternation with chant. The cantus firmus in "Tibi Christe splendor" has not been identified (it is not the standard chant), which suggests that Ercole's chapel used a different chant for this hymn that has yet to be discovered. Because this setting does not use the traditional chant as the cantus firmus, and because the traditional chant is in a different mode than this setting, a modern performance that alternated the traditional chant with this polyphonic setting would not be wholly satisfying. A practical solution to this problem could be to use the tenor of the polyphonic setting to sing verses 1 and 3, and thus maintain the balance between chant and polyphony that likely was the original method of performance.

Given the relatively simple nature of these hymns, the styles of the two composers are not radically different; nevertheless, there are some distinctions that

TABLE 2
Hymns by Martini and Brebis

Hymn	Feast	Tradition	Voices	Performing Requirements	Composers
Audi, benigne conditor	Weekdays in Lent	Italian	3	Double choir	?/Martini
Aures ad nostras	Sundays in Lent	Italian	3	Double choir	Brebis/Martini
Ave maris stella	Mary	Italian	4	Single choir	Martini
Deus tuorum militum (1)	Common of one martyr	Italian	3	Double choir	Brebis/Martini
Deus tuorum militum (2)	Common of one martyr	Italian	4	Single choir	Martini
Exultet celum laudibus	Common of Apostles	Italian	3	Double choir	Martini/Martini
Festum nunc celebre	Ascension	German	4	Single choir	Martini
Iste confessor	Common of a Confessor	Italian	3	Double choir	Martini/lacking
Jesu, corona virginum	Common of virgins	Italian	3	Double choir	Martini/lacking
Sanctorum meritis	Common of many martyrs	Italian	3	Double choir	Brebis/Martini
Tibi, Christe, splendor	St. Michael	Italian	4	Single choir	Martini
Vexilla regis	Passion Sunday	Italian	3	Double choir	Brebis/Martini

can be drawn.[10] In general, Martini's music is more sophisticated than Brebis's. Brebis favors nearly homophonic settings, with only a small amount of imitation between two voices; Martini's music is more contrapuntal and uses imitation more frequently, occasionally among all three voices. Martini's rhythmic structure is more complex than Brebis's, and he is more apt to have ties over the barline and brief changes in meter. Both composers use a variety of different types of cadences, although Martini likes the octave-leap cadence far more than Brebis.[11]

Ottaviano Petrucci published a volume of hymns in 1507 that contained at least one hymn by Martini ("Conditor alme syderum"). It has frequently been suggested that this collection, now lost, only contained hymns by Martini; indeed, it is often cited as "Hymnorum Lib. primus Io. Martini."[12] More recently, however, Stanley Boorman has suggested that it was not devoted solely to Martini but rather contained pieces by a variety of composers, and that the first setting happened to be by Martini. He suggests that the print was in choirbook format and that the title was, "Hymni de tempore et de sanctis liber primus."[13] Although we know that copies were once owned by Fernando Colon and the Fugger family, we do not have an inventory and so do not know whether the print contained other pieces by Martini, or if "Conditor alme syderum" was the only one.[14]

The Magnificats

The Magnificat was an important genre for Martini. Of the nine Magnificats in this edition, six are attributed to Martini, one to Brebis, and two are anonymous but may have been composed by either Martini or Brebis. The four settings in ModE M.1.11 appear as a unit (fols. 39r–42v) and are arranged in descending modal order (modes 8, 6, 3, and 1; whether this was intentional or coincidental is a matter for debate). They were probably double-choir settings in which the two choirs alternated verses, but the corresponding sections of ModE M.1.12 are missing. The fourteen Magnificats in VatS 15 (fols. 71v–160r) are arranged in modal order, with one to three settings in each tone. Martini's mode 3 and mode 4 settings are placed first in their respective modes. The eleven Magnificats in MunBS 3154 do not appear as a group but are spread out through the manuscript. Martini's four settings appear together, but not in modal order. Three of the four settings in ModE M.1.11 are "faulx bourdon"; one of them (Magnificat 3. toni [1]) has three written-out voices in addition to the rubric "faulx bourdon." None of the Magnificats that exist only in non-Modenese sources use faulx bourdon, suggesting that faulx bourdon was more accepted in Ferrara than elsewhere.

In most cases, the Magnificats in this edition have the intonation in the top voice, but in three settings it appears in the tenor (Magnificat 3. toni [2], and Magnificat 8. toni [2] and [3]). The Magnificat settings vary from the relatively short (e.g., Magnificat 8. toni [2]) to the comparatively long (Magnificat 6. toni). The shorter settings are either in faulx bourdon or use the same music for multiple verses; the longer settings are much more expansive, consisting of contrasting sections of imitation and homophony.

The Other Motets

Three of Martini's motets are settings of miscellaneous liturgical texts: "Ave decus virginale" sets verses 7 and 8 of the Marian sequence "Ave, virgo gratiosa"; "Da pacem, Domine" uses a benediction for peace as its text; and "Domine, non secundum" sets the tract for the mass used on Mondays, Wednesdays, and Fridays during Lent. Although "Ave decus virginale" clearly uses a cantus firmus, it is not derived from the chant for the sequence from which the text is taken. Both stanzas use the same cantus firmus—typical of the sequence—but with a change in meter and new polyphony around it. The cantus firmus, stated in the tenor, moves at the same speed as the other voices and is frequently imitated. "Da pacem, Domine" contains a strict canon between the altus and tenor, as indicated by the rubric "Tenor altus fuga." An embellished version of the chant is used as the basis of the canon, but it is imitated in the other voices as well and thus permeates the texture. "Domine, non secundum" uses the chant melody mainly in the superius, although it is sometimes stated in both the other voices as well. The presence of "Domine, non secundum" in ModE M.1.11 raises some interesting questions. It is one of the few pieces in this manuscript not composed for double choir. Furthermore, it is the only piece for use in the mass in a manuscript otherwise devoted to music for the office. Why is it here? Did it have a place in one of the office hours as performed in Ferrara? The text is of specifically Roman origin and settings were common at the papal chapel (the earliest settings are found in VatS 35, dating to ca. 1487–90, and the tradition continues into the sixteenth century). This is one of the few settings that did not originate in Rome and this forces us to ask why it was placed there. Was Ercole trying to compete with the pope, or perhaps prove his worthiness? In 1479 (just two years before this manuscript was compiled), Pope Sixtus IV—a long-time enemy of the Este family—wrote a bull in which he referred to Ercole as a rebel and traitor, excommunicated him, denied him his ducal dignity, his vicariate and all his fiefs, which devolved back to the Church, and released Ercole's subjects from their allegiance to him. Perhaps it was Ercole's hope to improve relations with the papacy that induced him to commission the composition of this work.

The two passions—"Non in die festo" (St. Matthew Passion) and "Jesum Nazarenum" (St. John Passion)—are both from ModE M.1.12 and are also among the few pieces not intended for double choir from this manuscript. Like "Domine, non secundum," the passions are not part of the office, and so their presence here is problematic; Kurt von Fischer suggests that they are there simply because of their novel character and the fact that other liturgical books would not readily accommodate them.[15] They are also the earliest extant polyphonic passions from Italy; the only earlier ones are of English origin and are found in London, British Library, MS Egerton 3307, dating from ca. 1430–40. Crowd scenes in both passions are written in polyphony with a cantus firmus that varies from simple two part settings (sometimes with the rubric "faulx bourdon," and sometimes without it[16]) to imitative sections written for eight parts. Individual characters are named in the manuscript and are usually differentiated by register according to their gender. The St. John Passion opens with the rubric "feria sexta," which specifies on what day it was to be performed.

The motets "Levate capita vestra" and "O beate Sebastiane" are in all likelihood very late motets: the earliest source of both is Petrucci's *Motetti libro quarto* (1505). The text of "Levate capita vestra" is cobbled together from various chants of First Vespers for Christmas, but the motet does not use any of the chants associated with those texts. Its exact liturgical use is uncertain, although John Brawley suggests that it may have been used in a procession.[17] This motet represents a significant change in Martini's musical style: it is strongly syllabic, avoiding melismatic passages, and uses paired duets, both imitative and non-imitative. Martini seems to have adopted these key elements of Josquin des Prez's style late in his career. The text of "O beate Sebastiane" is a plea for succor in time of plague, although it could also be used on the feast of St. Sebastian, 20 January. We do not know if Martini wrote this piece during a particular outbreak of the plague—there were several during his tenure in Ferrara; the one that lasted from 1482–84 was particularly virulent and tenacious—or whether he conceived of the motet in more general terms as one that could be used during any outbreak of disease. In any event, other composers also composed pieces beseeching St. Sebastian's help, including Guillaume Du Fay, Franchinus Gafurius, and Gaspar van Weerbeke; indeed, Weerbeke's motet—also found in Petrucci's *Motetti libro quarto*—uses the same text, and its tenor shares melodic material with Martini's setting. Although not as syllabic as "Levate capita vestra," "O beate Sebastiane" once again shows Josquin's influence in its use of paired duets and greater variety of texture.

The only source of the anonymous "Perfunde celi rore" is TrentC 91, which dates from 1472–77, placing it among the earliest motets in this edition. It most likely was written in 1473 for the wedding of Ercole I d'Este and Eleanora d'Aragona. Wolfgang Stephan was the first to attribute it to Martini, and that ascription has been accepted ever since.[18] In both halves of the motet, the tenor voice begins in longer note values but quickly picks up speed so that it moves at the same rate as the other voices. The tenor in the second half begins as a varied repetition of the opening of the first half (compare mm. 77–102 with mm. 5–13); after the opening phrase, however, it bears little resemblance to the tenor of the first half. At first blush, this might seem to be a tenor motet, but Julie Cumming has argued persuasively that it is indeed a free motet.[19] As with other pieces from TrentC 91, this motet uses imitation sparingly (see mm. 36–39 and 55–61), and only for two voices at a time. In this regard it is much like Martini's *Missa Cucu,* which also appears in TrentC 91 and which probably dates from roughly the same time. In only slightly later works such as *Missa Cela sans plus,* Martini uses imitation far more frequently and involves all the voices. Other features of "Perfunde celi rore" include infrequent changes in texture; long, melismatic phrases; infrequent and overlapped cadences; and an aesthetic in which the clear projection of the text was not of great concern.

The motet "Hercules omni memorandus evo" is Brebis's only known secular work. It is a celebratory motet in honor of Ercole that was copied into an older manuscript around 1472, placing it very close in time and style to "Perfunde celi rore." It is divided into two halves, with the second half about twice as long as the first; the tenor does not appear to have a cantus firmus, and although it occasionally moves in very long notes, most frequently it is fully integrated into the texture; it is melismatic with long phrases and overlapped cadences; and it uses imitation infrequently, usually in only two voices at a time (but see mm. 191–97, where it is used in all the voices). The text is telescoped among the voices, again suggesting that clear projection of the text was not of great concern. Brebis often varies the texture: each half begins with an extended introductory duet, and once the other voices have entered, there are frequent sections for only two or three voices.

The "Salve Regina" Problem

The "Salve Regina" on fols. 89r–93r of MunBS 3154 has an ascription that at first glance appears to read "Jo. m." Rudolf Gerber assumed this referred to Martini and published the motet along with two other securely attributed pieces.[20] Most subsequent scholars have accepted this attribution, including Thomas Noblitt, who edited the manuscript, and Lewis Lockwood and myself, who wrote and revised the *New Grove* article on Martini.[21] Brawley was the first to question the attribution,[22] and I now believe that the issue needs to be carefully re-examined.

Apart from the "Salve Regina," there are six pieces in MunBS 3154 attributed to Martini ("Ave maris stella," "Festum nunc celebre," and the Magnificats 3. toni [2], 4. toni, 6. toni, and 8. toni [1]), all copied by the same scribe, and all with the same form of his name in the attribution: "Jo. martini" (see plate 1). "Salve Regina," although copied by the same scribe as the Martini pieces, is attributed to what initially looks like "Jo. m." A closer inspection of the attribution reveals that the last initial is not an "m" but another letter, perhaps a lower case "a" (see plate 2). Brawley tentatively speculated that this ascription to "Jo. a" might refer to the Johannes Aulen who composed the "Salve virgo virginum" that appears in Petrucci's *Motetti libro quatro*.[23] This attribution is not stylistically apt, however, as the "Salve virgo virginum" is in late fifteenth-century style comparable to the generation of Josquin or Jacob Obrecht whereas the "Salve Regina" is in a mid-fifteenth-century style comparable to that of the previous generation. Although the work dates to a time when Martini was active, the scribe did not attribute it to him, and there is no reason to assume that Martini composed it. From a stylistic standpoint, it could have been composed by any one of a number of composers active between 1460–80.

Evaluation of the Sources

Martini's motets—both the securely attributed ones and those attributed to him by modern scholars—are preserved in nine manuscript sources and two printed anthologies. All but three of the sources originated in Italy: Martini's works in MunBS 3154 were copied in Innsbruck (and possibly Augsburg) between 1476–82, DresSL 1/D/505 was copied in or near Wittenberg between 1510–30, and BarcBC 454 was copied in Barcelona between 1520–25. Most of the sources contain only one or two motets by Martini; only three manuscripts contain more than two motets: VatS 15 has four motets; MunBS 3154 contains six motets; and ModE M.1.11–12 has ten, although some or all of the anonymous two- and three-part psalm settings as well as the two passions may be by Martini as well. Martini's motets did not circulate widely: only seven are not unica: six survive in two sources ("Ave maris stella," the Magnificats 3. toni [1], 4. toni, 6. toni, 8. toni [2], and "O beate Sebastiane") and one survives in three (Magnificat 3. toni [2]). The earliest source (TrentC 91) was copied in Trent ca. 1472–77, while the latest source (DresSL 1/D/505) was copied ca. 1510–30. The majority of the manuscripts were copied during his adult career.

By comparison, Brebis's motets circulated in a much smaller area, appearing in only two Ferrarese sources: ModE M.1.11–12 and ModE X.1.11. Many of his motets are hymns in which he composed the odd-numbered verses and Martini composed the even-numbered ones. Only two pieces—"Hercules omni memorandus evo" and a Magnificat—were composed by Brebis alone.

DresSL 1/D/505 was probably copied in or near Wittenberg and later brought to Annaberg and used at the Church of St. Anne.[24] It contains eight complete masses and seven individual mass movements; a large number of mass propers; various liturgical pieces including Magnificats, Te Deums, psalms, hymns, and a passion; more than thirty motets; one German-texted sacred piece; and three textless pieces. Most of the pieces are anonymous; Heinrich Isaac is the best-represented composer with seven works; Heinrich Finck has five pieces; Josquin has at least three; Antoine Brumel has three; Obrecht has at least two; and Alexander Agricola, Loyset Compère, Martini, Raber, Adam Rener, and Thomas Stoltzer all have one piece each.

The double-choir manuscript ModE M.1.11–12 dates from 1479–81.[25] It contains sixty-nine psalms for two to three voices, with the two choirs alternating verses; eight hymns similarly arranged; four Magnificats, also similarly arranged; two passions; and one tract. The only two composers named in the manuscript are Martini and Brebis; some of the hymns have the odd-numbered verses by Brebis and the even-numbered ones by Martini. Kanazawa has attributed one of the anonymous hymn sections to Brebis and another to Martini,[26] and there is a strong possibility that all of the remaining anonymous pieces in the manuscript are by these two composers. Someone has cut out the illuminated borders on the first folio of each manuscript and some illuminated capitals from the interior of ModE M.1.11. In addition, fourteen folios have been torn out of the middle of ModE M.1.12.[27]

The main layer of ModE X.1.11 was copied ca. 1440–48, with additions ca. 1450–60 and ca. 1471–80; more specifically, Lockwood dates the copying of the sole piece by Brebis—"Hercules omni memorandus evo"—to late 1471 or, more likely, 1472.[28] The repertory includes nine Magnificats, a Te Deum, a psalm, twenty-nine hymns, and ninety-one motets. Since the bulk of the repertory was copied by 1448, most of the composers are from the first half of the century. Du Fay is the best-represented composer, with at least forty-seven pieces; Dunstable has twenty-five pieces; Gilles Binchois has thirteen; Leonel Power has seven; Forest has four; Benoit has three; John Benet, Johannes Fedé, and Stone each have two; and Brebis and John Pyamour each have one. The latest pieces to be copied into the manuscript are the Brebis motet and four anonymous hymns.

MunBS 3154 was copied over a long period of time, from approximately 1466 to 1511.[29] It contains a variety of genres, including twenty-two masses plus fifteen individual mass movements or pairs; thirty-three mass propers; other liturgical pieces including Magnificats, hymns, and a psalm; two motet cycles that substitute for the mass ordinary; sixty-four motets; eight German or Dutch secular pieces; twenty textless pieces; and three fragmentary pieces. Martini, Isaac, and Obrecht are the best represented composers, with six pieces each; Josquin and Finck each have two pieces; Agricola, Antoine Busnoys, Nycasius Clibano, Compère, Du Fay, Antoine de Févin, Johannes de Salice, Jung, Raber, and Veye each have one piece; the majority of the pieces are anonymous. One of the pieces in this manuscript, "Salve Regina" (fols. 89r–93r), is often mistakenly attributed to Martini (see above).

TrentC 91 was copied in Trent between 1472 and 1477, and is the earliest source with a motet by Martini. It is one of seven large codices compiled in Trent between ca. 1430–77, which together contain more than fifteen hundred pieces in all genres. TrentC 91 was the last of these manuscripts to be copied; Peter Wright has shown that the earliest layer was copied ca. 1472–74 and the rest shortly thereafter, ca. 1474–77.[30] Martini is too young to be well represented in the Trent codices. In addition to "Perfunde celi rore," his only other securely attributed works in this source are *Missa Cucu* (the first piece in the manuscript) and the instrumental piece *La martinella*.

MilD 1 was copied in Milan ca. 1480–90 for use by the cathedral choir.[31] It was prepared under the direction of Franchinus Gaffurius, the *maestro di cappella* at the cathedral from 1484 until his death in 1522. It is the first of four large manuscripts compiled during Gafurius's tenure at the cathedral, and is devoted primarily to sacred music. It contains over a hundred motets, nearly two dozen Magnificats, nine liturgical pieces (hymns, a Sanctus, and a Te Deum), and two textless pieces. The composers represented in MilD 1 are primarily those who spent time at the court of Galeazzo Maria Sforza (r. 1466–76); Gafurius, Compère, and Weerbeke are especially well represented, but Binchois, Du Fay, Arnolfo Giliardi, Martini, and Johannes Pullois also have one or two pieces each. It is doubtful that Martini had composed his two Magnificats found in MilD 1 during his brief stay in the Sforza court cappella during 1474. Milan and Ferrara regularly exchanged music and musicians throughout most of Ercole's reign, however, and it would not have been difficult for the Sforzas or Gafurius to obtain Martini's music whenever they wanted it.

Two sources of Martini's motets now locate in Verona. VerBC 759 is the primary source of Martini's Magnificat 3. toni (2) and was probably copied in Verona mainly between 1480–90, with later additions.[32] It contains eight complete masses in addition to Magnificats, psalms, hymns, and motets. The bulk of the repertory is anonymous; the known composers include Barbingant, Giovanni Brocco, Marco Cara, Petrus Congeri, Du Fay, Josquin, Jean de Ockeghem,

Johannes de Quadris, and Johannes Tinctoris. VerBC 758 also was probably copied in Verona around 1500. It contains Magnificats, hymns, motets, a lauda, and three textless pieces. As with the earlier Verona source, most of the pieces are anonymous in VerBC 758; the composers known through concordances include Brumel, Compère, Josquin, Martini, Ninot le Petit, Conrad Rupsch, and Weerbeke.

VatS 15 contains three Magnificats by Martini; it is sometimes also listed as a source for "Salve Regina," but none of its "Salve Reginas" concord with the one sometimes attributed to Martini. It was probably copied in Rome between 1495–1500.[33] The manuscript contains Magnificats, hymns, and motets from many of the well-known composers of the time, including Agricola, Brumel, Busnoys, Compère, Du Fay, Isaac, Josquin, Martini, Marbrianus de Orto, Pullois, Johannes Regis, Antonius de Vinea, and Weerbeke.

BarcBC 454 was probably copied in Barcelona between 1520–25.[34] This manuscript contains three concordances to Petrucci's 1505[2], including two motets entitled "O beate Sebastiane," the first attributed to Martini in 1505[2] but to Moton (Jean Mouton) in BarcBC 454, and the second by Weerbeke. Emilio Ros-Fábregas suggests that the main scribe of BarcBC 454 (Anthoni Johan) copied directly from the Petrucci print and that he mistakenly copied the attribution to Moton from the index, where two pieces attributed to Moton appear very close to this motet's attribution to Jo. Martini.[35] The manuscript contains a variety of pieces, including masses, Magnificats, psalms, hymns, a lamentation, a passion, motets, Spanish pieces, and textless pieces. About half of the more than 120 pieces are anonymous; many of the composers were either Spanish or had spent time in Spain, including Juan de Anchieta, Matheo Flecha, Alonso Mondéjar, Pedro de Pastrana, Francisco de Peñalosa, and Ockeghem. Martini—who had no direct connection with Spain—was probably known only because his "O beate Sebastiane" had been published by Petrucci.

Petrucci published two prints that contain motets by Martini.[36] The first—*Motetti De Passione, De Cruce, De Sacramento, De Beata Virgine Et Huiusmodi B* (1503[1])—contains thirty-four motets and was published in choirbook format in Venice. The two composers best represented in this print are Josquin and Weerbeke, both with five motets; the other composers represented are Agricola, Regis, Brumel, Compère, Crispin van Stappen, Franci, Gregoire, Martini, Isaac, Pierre Moulu, Obrecht, Orto, Michele Pesenti, and Bertrandus Vaqueras; nine motets remain anonymous. This is the only source for Martini's "Ave decus virginale." The second—*Motteti libro quarto* (1505[2])—contains forty-five motets and was published as a set of four part books. The composers represented include Brumel and Johannes Ghiselin, each with five motets; Josquin, with four; Obrecht and Weerbeke, each with three; Erasmus Lapicida, Martini, Mouton, and Ninot, each with two; and Agricola, Aulen, Philippe Basiron, Bulkyn, Jheronimus de Clibano, Pierre de La Rue, Oberti, and Turplin, each with a single motet; nine motets are still anonymous. This is the only source for Martini's "Levate capita vestra."

Notes on Performance

Pitch in the fifteenth century was not fixed as it is now, and transposition up or down to suit the needs of the performing ensemble was common. Modern performers should feel free to do the same.

Performing ensembles in the fifteenth century were small. One singer on a part was very common, and ensembles averaging two or three on a part were normal. Larger ensembles were rare at this time.[37] The final chords at some cadences contain two pitches in a single part, giving these chords a richer, fuller texture. Depending on the number of singers per part, all these pitches could be sung, or the singers may choose whichever option they prefer.

Notes

1. Johannes Martini, *Masses,* ed. Elaine Moohan and Murray Steib, 2 vols., Recent Researches in the Music of the Middle Ages and Early Renaissance, vols. 34–35 (Madison, Wis.: A-R Editions, 1999), 1:vii–xi.

2. Lockwood, 172.

3. G. P. Calessi, "Ricerche sull'Accademia della morte di Ferrara," *Quadrivium* 16, no. 2 (1975): 17.

4. The most complete biography of Brebis can be found in Lockwood, 160–61.

5. See KanazawaP.

6. Lockwood, 252.

7. "For a book of vespers music for the chapel choir of our Signore [Ercole I d'Este], composed by Johannes Martini composer." See Charles Hamm and Ann Besser Scott, "A Study and Inventory of the Manuscript Modena, Biblioteca Estense, alph.X.1.11 (ModB)," *Musica Disciplina* 26 (1972): 110; and Adriano Franceschini, *Artisti a Ferrara in età umanistica e rinascimento: testimonianze archivistiche* (Ferrara: Gabiele Corbo, 1993–97), entry no. 275e.

8. Tom R. Ward, *The Polyphonic Office Hymn, 1400–1520: A Descriptive Catalogue,* Renaissance Manuscript Studies, vol. 3 (Neuhausen-Stuttgart: American Institute of Musicology, 1980), 16–17.

9. Rifkin, 318–19.

10. Lockwood, 252; Masakata Kanazawa, "Martini and Brebis at the Estense Chapel," in *Essays Presented to Myron Gilmore,* ed. Sergio Bertelli and Gloria Ramakus (Florence: La Nuova Italia Editrice, 1978), 426.

11. For example, in the hymn "Aures ad nostras," composed jointly by Brebis and Martini, Brebis does not use any octave-leap cadences, but Martini uses three (mm. 39, 46, and 59).

12. Claudio Sartori, *Bibliografia delle opere musicali stampate da Ottaviano Petrucci* (Florence: Leo S. Olschki, 1948), 128.

13. Stanley Boorman, *Ottaviano Petrucci: Catalogue Raisonne* (Oxford: Oxford University Press, 2006), 667–68.

14. Ibid., 667.

15. Kurt von Fischer, *Essays in Musicology,* trans. Carl Skoggard, ed. Tamara S. Evans (New York: Graduate School and University Center, City University of New York, 1989), 30.

16. In this edition, a faulx bourdon part has only been added where it is specifically called for in the manuscript source.

17. Brawley, 1:67.

18. Stephan, 65; see also Benvenuto Disertori, *Johannes Martini: Magnificat e messe,* AMMM 12 (1964), 88; and Lockwood, 258.

19. Julie E. Cumming, *The Motet in the Age of Du Fay* (Cambridge: Cambridge University Press, 1999), 283.

20. Gerber, 4.

21. Noblitt, 81:11–24; *The New Grove Dictionary of Music and Musicians,* 2nd ed., s.v. "Martini, Johannes," by Lewis Lockwood and Murray Steib.

22. Brawley, 1:65–66.

23. Ibid., 1:66.

24. Wolfram Steunde, *Untersuchungen zur mitteldeutschen Musiküberlieferung und Musikpflege im 16. Jahrhunderts* (Leipzig: C. F. Peters, 1978).

25. Lockwood, 221.

26. KanazawaP.

27. Elaine Moohan, "Sources of Sacred Music for the Chapel Choir of Ercole I d'Este (1471–1505) Duke of Ferrara and the Masses of Johannes Martini" (Ph.D. diss., University of Manchester, 1993), 68.

28. Lockwood, 55.

29. Thomas Noblitt, "Das Chorbuch des Nikolaus Leopold (München, Staatsbibliothek, Mus. Ms. 3154): Repertorium," *Die Musikforschung* 27 (1974): 36–56; see also Rifkin, 239–351.

30. Peter Wright, "Paper Evidence and the Dating of Trent 91," *Music and Letters* 76 (1995): 504.

31. A facsimile of MilD 1 has been published as volume 12 of the series Renaissance Music in Facsimile (New York: Garland, 1987).

32. Masakata Kanazawa, "Two Vespers Repertories from Verona, ca. 1500," *Rivista Italiana di Musicologia* 10 (1975): 156.

33. Richard Sherr, *Papal Music Manuscripts in the Late Fifteenth and Early Sixteenth Centuries.* Renaissance Manuscript Studies, vol. 5 (Neuhausen-Stuttgart: American Institute of Musicology, 1996), 58–67.

34. Ros-Fábregas, 87–88.

35. Ibid., 311–12 and 350.

36. For more information on the Petrucci prints, see Boorman, *Ottaviano Petrucci,* 496–503 and 584–91.

37. David Fallows, "Specific Information on the Ensembles for Composed Polyphony, 1400–1474," in *Studies in Performance of Late Mediaeval Music,* ed. Stanley Boorman (Cambridge: Cambridge University Press, 1983), 109–59.

Critical Commentary

Editorial Methods

Each motet has been transcribed from a single source, and concordant sources were used as necessary to correct scribal errors. Variants in the concordant sources are listed in the critical notes. For those seven motets that exist in multiple sources, a variety of criteria were used to determine which manuscript to use as the primary source, including: the number and kind of errors, their proximity in both time and place to Martini, and their completeness (for example, ModE M.1.12 is missing some folios in the middle, and as a result, Magnificat 3. toni [1] contains only the odd-numbered verses in ModE M.1.11).

In this edition, note values have been reduced by half, modern clefs are used, and barlines have been added to mark off measures of one breve duration. In the sections of chant, barlines that appear in the original sources are retained. Double barlines are added at the borders between choral sections. Incipits are provided at the beginning of each motet that include the name of the voice part, its clef, key signature, initial mensuration sign, and the first note or ligature as found in the primary source. No incipit is provided for a voice part if the voice entry is delayed for more than ten measures. "Perfunde celi rore" has a longer incipit than usual in order to show where the fugal voice enters. When mensuration signs change in the primary source, the originals are provided above the affected staves. Voices that are marked "tacet" in the original source are shown with whole-measure rests in this edition.

Faulx bourdon is not written out in the original sources but is marked with the rubric "faulx bourdon." In this edition, it has been realized from the rubric on a full-sized staff. In places where faulx bourdon alternates with regular three-voice writing, the part is labeled either as "faulx bourdon" or "Tenor" or "Contratenor" to avoid confusion. Faulx bourdon was used regularly in choir 1 of ModE M.1.11–12, but it was never designated in choir 2. Although some of the two-voiced sections of the psalm settings in choir 2 could be performed in faulx bourdon, I have chosen not to realize them this way, as there is ample justification that they were not so performed.

The scoring of the two passions requires some explanation. The soloists who sing the parts of individual characters should be part of the choir and therefore also sing the chant portions. In the original source, each character's part was given on its own staff and alternated either with another character or the choir singing chant. In the edition, I have combined characters by voice range, so that in "Jesum Nazarenum" (St. John Passion), for example, the top staff represents three different characters (Turba 1, Pontifices et ministri 1, and Ancilla) who would be sung by three different people in performance.

All of the chant incipits in the psalms and canticles, as well as in the chant in the two passions, are found in the original sources. Slurs are used to indicate neumes in the chant. The chants found in Magnificat 3. toni (2) are found in the manuscript source; however, those in Magnificats 1. toni, 8. toni (2), and 8. toni (3) have been editorially supplied from modern chant books. In the Magnificats, where the chant melody repeats with a differing number of syllables, parentheses surround reciting pitches needed for one repetition but not for another. The clef used in the chant sections is that of the original. The barlines in the chant sections generally follow the original manuscripts; the chant is ametrical and the barlines do not imply a metrical grouping. In the passions, there is a double barline at the end of each character's section; in the one place where the scribe left it out I have added it and mentioned it in the critical notes. Furthermore, the scribe used double barlines in the middle of a character's chant when there is text left out from the Bible.

Accidentals occurring in the primary source are placed in the staff, and editorial accidentals are indicated above the staff. All source accidentals are reported where they occur regardless of whether their meaning is superfluous by modern notational standards. In this edition, editorial accidentals, or *musica ficta,* have been supplied above the staff in order to raise the leading tone at cadences, to obviate cross-relations, and to avoid tritones, especially those that occur melodically. *Musica ficta* apply only to the notes to which they are connected; they do not affect notes of the same pitch class that may occur later in the measure. The application of *musica ficta* is not always clear cut; in most cases, the solution was simple and straightforward, but a few examples were far more complicated. Sometimes two solutions seemed equally good, other times no solution seemed completely adequate. In all cases, I have indicated what I believe to be the simpler solution, but performers should feel free to experiment with other possibilities.[1]

Pitches notated in ligatures in the primary source are marked off with square brackets above the staff, and coloration is indicated by broken brackets. Fermatas are used only where they appear in the primary source.

In the original sources, capitalization is used only for the first word of a section, and punctuation, when it occurs at all, is used only at the ends of sections; in this edition, capitalization and punctuation have been modernized. One of the most frustrating problems facing editors of fifteenth-century motets is trying to fit the text to the music, as most of the manuscript sources for this music are especially parsimonious with the application of text to all voices. In pieces that are essentially syllabic (such as the psalm settings), the solution is usually fairly straightforward, however many of Martini's and Brebis's motets are not syllabic. Text underlay varies considerably between sources, and at the best of times the scribe gives only a rough idea of the phrase underlay, paying little or no attention to the underlay of individual syllables. Specific hints about phrase underlay have been followed whenever possible, but the position of individual syllables in the underlay in this edition should be considered editorial, and users should feel free to adjust the details according to their own judgment and sense of style.[2] The critical notes do not report all of the different details of underlay in all of the sources; scholars and performers wishing to pursue this aspect will need to consult the sources themselves.

With only a few exceptions, all of the texts are standard; some of the pieces have the complete text only in the top voice while the other voices have anything from incipits to nearly complete text; a few pieces, mainly the psalms, have complete text in all voices. For all of these pieces, any text in angled brackets is simply missing from that voice part and is supplied by the top voice. Occasionally, the scribe left out a word in all the voices from a standard text and that has also been put in angled brackets.

There are two exceptions to these practices. The first is Martini's "Perfunde celi rore." This work does not have a standard text, but the text is complete in the top voice and nearly complete in the others, so angled brackets have been used here as well. The second exception is Brebis's "Hercules omni memorandus evo," which has a text written for a specific occasion. The text that was used was edited by Leofranc Holford-Strevens and has some missing text that he has speculated on, as noted in the critical notes. These speculations have been placed in square brackets (both involve the tenor: "bene" in mm. 164–65, and "Hercules" in mm. 187–92).

In this edition, I have chosen to retain the spellings found in the original sources rather than using classical Latin spellings. Latin was continually evolving from its beginning, through the Roman empire, throughout the very long Middle Ages, and up to the present. By the time we get to the sources used in this edition, it had been around for more then a millennium and a half. It was not until the very late fifteenth and especially the sixteenth centuries that there arose the belief that it was necessary to go back to Roman Empire vocabulary and grammar. The medieval spellings were not confined to music sources but were found everywhere, including contemporary Bibles and liturgical books: these were the preferred spellings at this time. Although spelling could vary very slightly from scribe to scribe, they tended to be more consistent than we sometimes give them credit, and furthermore, eighty-one of the ninety-eight pieces in this edition were copied by the same scribe. Even more important is that the different spellings usually had a profound effect on the pronunciation of these words. As an example, the word "mihi" in classical Latin was usually spelled "michi" in the fifteenth century, and it is this spelling that occurs in every occurrence of this word in all of the musical sources used in this edition. In the first spelling, the "h" would be pronounced much like the "h" in "hat," but in the second, the "ch" would be pronounced like the "ch" in "character." By retaining the original spelling, I am hoping that singers will experiment with original pronunciation.

When I co-edited the masses of Martini, I was convinced that words should not be broken by rests in the music, a philosophy that required much text repetition. Although this was true for much sixteenth-century music, I am no longer convinced that this is wholly applicable to music in the fifteenth century. Therefore, in this edition I have been far more willing to have singers sing a single word to long melismas that contain short rests.

Translations

The translations of the psalms and canticles are taken from the Douai English Bible; all other translations are my own unless otherwise noted.

Critical Notes

Voice-part abbreviations are A = Altus, B = Bassus, CT = Contratenor, S = Superius, T = Tenor. Pitches are given according to the system in which c′ = middle C.

1. *Audi, benigne conditor*

Primary sources. ModE M.1.11, fol. 34v. ModE M.1.12, fol. 34v, Io Martini.

Use. Hymn for weekdays in Lent.

Modern editions. Brawley, 2:88–89. KanazawaP, 2:192–93. Ward, 533–35.

Text sources. AH, 2:42. AH, 51:53–55. Walpole, 320–21.

Text

Audi, benigne conditor,
Nostras preces cum fletibus,
In hoc sacro jejunio
Fusas quadragenario.
Scrutator alme cordium,
Infirma tu scis virium,
Ad te reversis exhibe,
Remissionis gratiam.
Multum quidem peccavimus,
Sed parce confitentibus;
Ad laudem tui nominis
Confer medellam languidis.
Sic corpus extra conteri
Dona per abstinentiam,
Jejunet ut mens sobria
A labe prorsus criminum.
Presta, beata trinitas,
Concede, simplex unitas
Ut fructuosa sint tuis
Jejuniorum munera.

* * *

Listen, kind Creator,
to our prayers full of weeping
during this sacred time of fasting
spread over forty days.
Nurturing examiner of hearts,
you know the weakness of our resolve,
show the grace of pardon
to those who return to you.
We have sinned many times indeed,
but spare those who are repentant;
to the praise of your name
bestow healing to the sick.
Thus allow the body to be chastised
from without through abstinence,
let it fast so that a sober mind
thoroughly [escapes] the disgrace of sin.
Grant, blessed Trinity,
allow, single Unity,
that these offerings of fasting
may be valuable to you.

2. *Aures ad nostras*

Primary sources. ModE M.1.11, fol. 35r, Brebis. ModE M.1.12, fol. 35r, Io Martini.

Use. Hymn for Sundays in Lent.

Modern edition. Brawley, 2:90–92.

Text sources. AH, 2:83–84. AH, 51:61–63.

Text

Aures ad nostras
Deus, inclina pietate sola,
Supplicum vota suscipe, precamur
Famuli tui.
Respice clemens solio de sancto
Vultu sereno, lampadas illustra
Lumine tuo, tenebras depelle
Pectore nostro.
Crimina laxa pietate multa,
Ablue sordes, vincula disrumpe,
Parce peccatis, releva jacentes
Dextera tua.
Te sine tetro mergimur profundo,
Labimur alta sceleris sub unda;
Brachio tuo trahamur ad clara
Sidera celi.
Christe, lux vera, bonitas et vita,
Gaudium mundi, pietas immensa,
Qui nos a morte roseo salvasti
Sanguine tuo,
Insere tuum, petimus, amorem
Mentibus nostris, fidei refunde
Lumen eternum, caritatis auge
Dilectionem.
Tu nobis dona fontem lacrimarum
Jejuniorum fortia ministra,
Vitia carnis milia retunde
Framea tua.
Procul a nobis perfidus absistat
Satan a tuis viribus confractus,
Sanctus asistat spiritus a tua
Sede dimissus.
Gloria Deo sit eterno patri,
Sit tibi semper, genitoris nate,
Cum quo equalis spiritus per cuncta
Secula regnat. Amen.

* * *

Turn your divine ears to our prayers,
Lord, in your goodness alone,
accept your servants' prayers for mercy,
we beseech you.

Look down, O merciful one, from your throne
with holy and serene countenance, illuminate
the sun with your light, drive away the darkness
from our soul.
Punish our crimes, extend divine mercy,
cleanse our impurities, break our bonds,
have mercy on our sins, relieve the helpless
by your right hand.
Without you we are sunk to the horrible depths,
we sink deep under a wave of misfortune;
we would be pulled by your arm
to the bright, starry heaven.
Christ, true light, benevolence and life,
joy of the world, boundless charity,
who saved us from death
by his rose colored blood.
Plant your love, we beseech you,
in our minds, restore eternal light
to the faithful, extend love
to the charitable.
Spare us a fountain of tears,
provide strength to the weak,
quell the thousand imperfections of the flesh
by your sword.
May deceitful Satan withdraw broken
far away from us by your resolve,
let the Holy Spirit take up position by your side
when he has been sent away.
Glory be to God the eternal father,
glory be to him forever, born of the father,
together with the Holy Spirit, equal in status,
He reigns forever. Amen.

3. Ave maris stella

Primary source.   VerBC 758, fols. 58v–59r.

Concordant sources.   MunBS 3154, fol. 153v, Jo. Martini. MunBS 3154, fol. 253v.

Use.   Hymn for the Annunciation.

Modern editions.   Brawley, 2:111–12. Gerber, 19–20. Noblitt, 81:195–96. *MGG* 9, Tafel 56 (facsimile).

Text sources.   AH, 2:39. AH, 51:140–42.

Text

Ave maris stella,
Dei mater alma
Atque semper virgo,
Felix celi porta.
Sumens illud Ave
Gabrielis ore,
Funda nos in pace,
Mutans Eve nomen.
Solve vincla reis,
Profer lumen cecis,
Mala nostra pelle,
Bona cuncta posce.
Monstra te esse matrem,
Sumat per te precem,
Qui pro nobis natus
Tulit esse tuus.
Virgo singularis,
Inter omnes mitis,
Nos culpis solutos
Mites fac et castos.
Vitam presta puram,
Iter para tutum,
Ut videntes Jesum
Semper colleatemur.
Sit laus Deo patri,
Summo Christo decus,
Spiritui sancto
Tribus honor unus.

* * *

Hail, star of the sea,
kindly mother of God
yet always a virgin,
happy door of heaven.
Accepting that Hail
from Gabriel's lips,
establish us in peace,
transforming the name of Eve.
Loosen these earthly fetters,
bring light to the blind,
drive away our troubles,
intercede for all good things.
Show yourself to be a mother,
may he take up our prayers through you,
who was born for us
who suffered to be yours.
Remarkable Virgin,
more gentle than any other,
make us free of our sins,
mild and pure.
Render the good life,
provide a safe road,
so that seeing Jesus
we may rejoice together forever.
May there be praise to God the Father,
the greatest honor to Christ,
to the Holy Spirit
a single honor to all three.

Comment.   In VerBC 758, the second verse is underlaid in all voices, perhaps implying an alternatim performance in which the first verse would be sung in chant. In MunBS 3154, the first verse is underlaid in the S and T, along with an incipit in the B, on fol. 153v; no text whatsoever is given on fol. 253v.

Variants in MunBS 3154.   Variants occur in both Munich versions unless otherwise noted. M. 1, A, note 1 to m. 2, note 5, dotted semibreve d′, semiminim c′, semiminim b, semibreve a, minim g, minim b, minim c′, semibreve d′, minim c′. M. 2, B, notes 1–2, semibreve g. M. 8, S, notes 2–3, no ligature on fol. 253v only. M. 8, T, notes 3–4, ligature on fol. 153v only. M. 14, S, note 1 to m. 15, note 2, not colored. M. 14, S, note 3 to m. 15, note 1, no ligature on fol. 153v only. M. 15, T, note 3 to m. 16, note 2, no ligature. M. 15, A, notes 1–2, ligature. M. 17, A, note 2, semibreve g on fol. 153v only. M. 17, A, notes 1–2, ligature. M. 18, A, note 2, minim a. M. 18, B, notes 2–4, minim f, semibreve d ligated to semibreve A. M. 18, T, notes 3–4, ligature. M. 19, A, notes 1–3, semibreve f, semibreve a, ligated, minim b, minim a. M. 20, A, note 3, minim d′. M. 20, B, notes 1–2, no ligature on fol. 253v only. M. 21, A, notes 2–3, dotted minim d′, semiminim c′. M. 22, S, note 1, missing semibreve a′ on fol. 153v only. M. 22, B, notes 4–5, not minor color. M. 23, A, note 1 to m. 25, note 2, semibreve rest, semibreve rest, semibreve d, semibreve e ligated to dotted minim f, semiminim g in minor color, minim a, minim b, semibreve c′. M. 24, B, notes 3–4, minim B. M. 25, T, note 1 to m. 26, note 4, not colored. M. 25, T, note 2 to m. 26, note 1, no ligature. M. 27, T, note 1, color on fol. 153v only. M. 28, T, note 3 to m. 29, note 1, colored semibreve g, semibreve rest, on fol. 253v only. M. 28, T, note 3 to m. 29, note 1, semibreve g, semibreve g, on fol. 153v only. M. 28, B, notes 1–3, semibreve e ligated to dotted semibreve c. M. 29, A, note 5 to m. 30, note 3, minim c′, minim a, minim d′, minim c′. M. 30, B, notes 1–2, minim rest, minim d, minim e, minim c. M. 32, B, note 1, long d, long a, on fol. 153v only. M. 32, B, note 1, long D on fol. 253v only.

4. *Deus tuorum militum* (1)

Primary sources. ModE M.1.11, fol. 37r, Brebis. ModE M.1.12, fol. 37r, Io Martini.

Use. Hymn for the common of one martyr.

Modern editions. Brawley, 2:99–101. KanazawaP, 2:189–91. Lockwood, 252–54.

Text sources. AH, 2:76. AH, 51:130. Walpole, 386.

Text

Deus tuorum militum
Sors et corona, premium,
Laudes canentes martiris,
Absolve nexu criminis.
Hic nempe mundi gaudia,
Et blandimenta noxia,
Caduca rite deputans,
Pervenit ad celestia.
Poenas cucurrit fortiter
Et substulit viriliter,
Pro te efundens sanguinem

Eterna dona possidet.
Ob hoc precatu supplici
Te possimus, piissime,
In hoc triumpho martiris
Dimite noxam servulis.
Laus et perhepnis gloria
Deo patri et filio,
Sancto simul paraclito
In seculorum secula.

* * *

God of your soldiers,
[their] fortune, crown, and reward,
free from the bonds of crime
those who sing the martyr's praises.
Without doubt, this man, duly pruning
the harmful delights and fleeting pleasures
of the world,
reaches heaven.
He bravely faced torture
and endured it like a man,
in pouring out his blood for you
he obtains eternal reward.
Through this prayer of supplication
we implore you, most holy one,
on this triumph of the martyr
free your unworthy servants from harm.
Praise and eternal glory [be]
to God the Father and the Son
together with the Holy Spirit
for ever and ever.

5. *Deus tuorum militum* (2)

Primary source. ModE X.1.11, fols. 78v–79r.

Attribution. Rifkin, 318–19.

Use. Hymn for the common of one martyr.

Text source. See no. 4 above.

Text. See no. 4 above.

Notes. M. 10, A, note 1, a brief passage has been crossed out: minim c′, minim d′, dotted minim f′, semiminim g′, minim a′; the first note should not have been crossed out. M. 10, A, note 2, minim d′. M. 28, A, notes 1–2, rhythm is minim d′, minim b; this creates an unusually sharp dissonance on beat 2.

6. *Exultet celum laudibus*

Primary sources. ModE M.1.11, fol. 36v, Io Martini. ModE M.1.12, fol. 36v, Io Martini.

Use. Hymn for the common of Apostles.

Modern edition. Brawley, 2:96–97.

Text sources. AH, 2:74. AH, 51:125–26.

Text

Exultet celum laudibus,
Resultet terra gaudiis,
Apostolorum gloriam
Sacra canunt solemnia.
Vos, seculi justi judices
Et vera mundi lumina,
Votis precamur cordium,
Audite preces supplicum.
Qui celum verbo clauditis
Serasque ejus solvitis,
Nos a peccatis omnibus
Solvite jusu, quesumus.
Quorum precepto subditur
Salus et langor omnium
Sanate egros moribus
Nos redentes virtutibus,
Ut cum judex advenerit
Christus in fine seculi,
Nos sempiterni gaudii
Faciat esse compotes.
Deo patri sit gloria
Ejusque soli filio
Cum spiritu paraclito
Et nunc et in perpetuum.

* * *

Let heaven rejoice with praises,
let earth echo with joy,
let the holy and solemn sing
the glory of the Apostles.
You, just judges of the age
and true lights of the world,
we beseech you with vows of the heart,
hear our prayers of supplication.
You who close heaven
and loosen its bars with a word,
release us of all our sins
by your command, we implore.
The health and sickness of all
is subject to your command,
heal us who are sick in our habits,
restoring us to strength.
So that, when Christ comes
as judge at the end of time,
he will make us participants in
eternal joy.
Glory be to God the Father
and his only Son
with the Holy Spirit
now and in perpetuity.

7. *Festum nunc celebre*

Primary source. MunBS 3154, fols. 150v–151r, Jo. Martini.

Use. Hymn for the Ascension.

Modern editions. Brawley, 2:113–15. Noblitt, 81:188–89.

Text source. AH, 50:192–93.

Text

Festum nunc celebre magnaque gaudia,
Compellunt animos carmina promere,
Cum Christus solium scandit ad arduum,
Celorum pius arbiter.

* * *

Now the festive and great holiday
compels our spirits to bring out songs of joy
as Christ, the holy witness, alone ascends
the heights of heaven.

Note. M. 1, B, labeled "Bassa."

8. *Iste confessor*

Primary source. ModE M.1.11, fol. 38r, Io. Martini.

Use. Hymn for the common of Confessors.

Modern edition. Brawley, 2:105.

Text sources. AH, 2:77. AH, 51:134–35.

Text

Iste confessor Domini sacratus,
Festa plebs cujus celebrat per orbem,
Hodie letus meruit secreta
Scandere celi.
Ad sacrum cujus tumullum frequenter
Membra languentum modo sanitati,
Quolibet morbo fuerint gravata,
Restituuntur.

* * *

The holy Confessor of the Lord,
whose feast day people celebrate throughout the world,
on this day deserved to joyously ascend
to a special place in heaven.
The holy place at whose grave,
sick limbs only recently afflicted
by whatever disease, now were often
restored to health.

9. *Jesu, corona virginum*

Primary source. ModE M.1.11, fol. 38v, Io Martini.

Use. Hymn for the common of virgins.

Modern edition. Brawley, 2:106–7.

Text sources. AH, 2:78. AH, 50:20–21. Walpole, 112–14.

Text

Jesu, corona virginum,
Quem mater illa concipit,
Que sola virgo peperit,
Hec vota clemens accipe.
Quocumque pergis, virgines
Secuntur, atque laudibus
Post te canentes cursitant
Hymnosque dulces personant.

* * *

Jesus, crown of virgins,
whom that mother conceives,
the only virgin who gave birth,
merciful one, accept these prayers.
Wherever you go, virgins
follow, and with praises
they run after you singing,
and they make sweet hymns resound.

Comment. Only the odd-numbered verses are set because the corresponding page in ModE M.1.12 is missing, making this hymn incomplete. Line 3 has the word "peperit" instead of the more standard "parturit," but this does not significantly alter the meaning.

10. Sanctorum meritis

Primary sources. ModE M.1.11, fol. 37v, Brebis. ModE M.1.12, fol. 37v.

Use. Hymn for the common of many martyrs.

Modern editions. Brawley, 2:102–4. Ward, 536–39.

Text sources. AH, 2:75. AH, 50:204–5.

Text

Sanctorum meritis inclita gaudia,
Pangamus, socii, gestaque fortia,
Nam gliscit animus promere cantibus,
Victorum genus optimum.
Hi sunt, quos retinens mundus inhorruit,
Ipsum nam sterili flore peraridum,
Sprevere penitus teque secuti sunt,
Rex Christe bone, celitus.
Hi pro te furias atque ferocia
Calcarunt hominum sevaque verbera,
Cessit his lacerans fortiter ungula
Nec carpsit penetralia.
Ceduntur gladiis, more bidentium
Non murmur resonat, non querimonia,
Sed corde tacito mens bene conscia
Conservat patientiam.
[Que vox, que poterit lingua retexere,
Que tu martiribus munera preparas?
Rubri nam fluido sanguine laureis
Ditantur bene fulgidis.]
Te, trina deitas unaque, poscimus,
Ut culpas abluas, noxia subtrahas,
Des pacem famulis, nos quoque gloriam
Per cuncta tibi secula.

* * *

Companions, let us compose poems about the joys,
celebrated merits, and brave deeds of the saints,
for the soul is elated to reveal through poetry
this noblest race of victors.
They are the ones the world steadfastly inveighs against,
for they deeply despise the dried up, sterile flower
and have followed you,
O Christ, good and heavenly king.
For you they have spurned the madness and even the ferocity
of men and their cruel blows,
the powerful, mutilating hooks have yielded to them
but not torn their innermost being.
They have been slain by swords, like lambs
not a murmur nor a complaint is heard,
but with kindness in his heart and a quiet conscience
he remains patient.
What voice, what tongue will be able to undo
what you prepare for the funeral rites of the martyrs?
For as their blood flows red
may they be given a gleaming crown of laurels.
We beseech you, three gods in one,
wash away our faults, rescue us from harm,
give peace to your servants, and also glory,
for ever and ever.

11. Tibi, Christe, splendor

Primary source. ModE X.1.11, fols. 79v–80r.

Attribution. Rifkin, 318–19.

Use. Hymn for the feast of St. Michael (29 Sept.).

Text source. AH, 50:207–8.

Text

Tibi, Christe, splendor patris,
Vita, virtus cordium,
In conspectu angelorum
Votis voce psallimus,
Alternates concrepando
Melos damus vocibus.
Collaudamus venerantes
Omnes celi milites,
Sed precipue primatem
Celestis exercitus
Michalem in virtute
Conterentem zabulum.
Quo custode procul pelle,

Rex Christe piissime,
Omne nefas inimici,
Mundos corde et corpore
Paradiso redde tuo
Nos sola clementia.
Gloriam patri melodis
Personemus vocibus,
Gloriam Christo canamus,
Gloriam paraclito,
Qui Deus trius et unus
Extat ante secula. Amen.

* * *

For you, O Christ, splendor of the Father,
life and virtue of hearts,
in the sight of angels
we raise our voice in prayer,
alternately singing
we give voice to the song.
We praise with veneration
all the soldiers heaven,
but especially the head
of the heavenly army,
Michael, by virtue of
[his] crushing the devil.
With him as protector, drive far away,
O Christ, most faithful king,
all unfriendly, wicked people,
clean of heart and body
give us back your paradise
by your clemency alone.
Let us sing songs
to the glory of the Father,
let us sing to the glory of Christ,
and the glory of the Holy Spirit,
which God, three and one,
exists before time. Amen.

12. *Vexilla regis*

Primary sources. ModE M.1.11, fol. 35v, Brebis. ModE M.1.12, fol. 35v, Io. Martini.

Use. Hymn for Passion Sunday.

Modern edition. Brawley, 2:93–95.

Text sources. AH, 2:45. AH, 50:74–75. Walpole, 173–77.

Text

Vexilla regis prodeunt,
Fulget crucis misterium,
Quo carne carnis conditor
Suspensus est patibulo.
Quo vulneratus insuper
Mucrone dire lancee,
Ut nos lavaret crimine,
Manavit unda et sanguine.
Impleta sunt, que concinit
David fidelis carmine
Dicens in nationibus:
"Regnavit a ligno Deus."
Arbor decora et fulgida,
Ornata regis purpura,
Electa digno stipite
Tam sancta membra tangere.
Beata cujus brachiis
Seculi pependit pretium,
Statera facta [est] corporis
Predam tulitque tartari.
O crux, ave, spes unica,
Hoc passionis tempore.
Auge piis justitiam
Reisque dona veniam.
Te, summa Deus Trinitas,
Collaudet omnis spiritus:
Quos per crucis misterium
Salvas, rege per secula.

* * *

The banners of the king go forth,
the mystery of the cross shines brightly,
where, in the flesh, the creator of flesh
is hung from the gibbet.
Where, in addition, wounded
by the dreadful point of a sword,
water and blood poured forth
in order to cleanse us of our sins.
What David sang in truthful songs
is now fulfilled,
saying to all people
"God has reigned from the wood."
Beautiful and gleaming tree,
adorned with the king's purple,
chosen from a trunk
worthy to bear such sacred limbs.
Blessed tree from whose branches
hung the ransom of the world,
it was made a balance for his body
and carried away the prey of hell.
Hail, cross, our only hope,
in this time of the Passion.
Extend justice to the holy
and grant pardon to the guilty.
You, God, supreme Trinity,
let every spirit praise:
those whom you save through the mysteries of the cross,
rule for ever.

Note. M. 21, CT, note 1, semibreve rest should be a minim rest.

13. Magnificat 1. toni

Primary source. ModE M.1.11, fol. 42v.

Text source. Luke 1:46–55.

Text

1. Magnificat anima mea Dominum.
2. Et exsultavit spiritus meus in Deo salutari meo.
3. Quia respexit humilitatem ancile sue: ecce enim ex hoc beatam me dicent omnes generationes.
4. Quia fecit michi magna qui potens est: et sanctum nomen ejus.
5. Et misericordia ejus a progenie in progenies timentibus eum.
6. Fecit potentiam in brachio suo: dispersit superbos mente cordis sui.
7. Deposuit potentes de sede, et exaltavit humiles.
8. Esurientes implevit bonis: et divites dimisit inanes.
9. Suscepit Israel puerum suum, recordatus misericordie sue.
10. Sicut locutus est ad patres nostros, Abraham, et semini ejus in secula.
11. Gloria Patri, et Filio, et Spiritui Sancto.
12. Sicut erat in principio, et nunc, et semper, et in secula seculorum. Amen.

* * *

My soul magnifies the Lord.
And my spirit has exulted in God my Savior.
Because he has noticed the humility of his handmaiden: behold from henceforth all generations will call me blessed.
Because he who is powerful has made me great: and holy is his name.
And his mercy is on those who fear him, from generation to generation.
He showed strength in his arm; he scattered the proud in the conceit of their heart.
He put down the mighty from their seat and exalted the humble.
He has filled the hungry with good things: and dismissed the wealthy with nothing.
He supported Israel, his children, calling to mind his mercy.
As he said to our fathers, Abraham, and his seed forever.
Glory be to the Father, the Son, and the Holy Spirit.
As it was in the beginning, is now, and ever shall be, and world without end. Amen.

Comment. Setting of the odd verses only; even verses missing.

14. Magnificat 3. toni (1)

Primary source. VatS 15, fols. 91v–95r.

Concordant source. ModE M.1.11, fols. 41v–42r, Io. Martini.

Modern editions. Brawley, 2:32–39. KanazawaP, 2:194–95. Lerner, 55 [partial score].

Text source. See no. 13 above.

Text. See no. 13 above.

Comments. The text of verse 9 is placed beneath the text of verse 3 in ModE M.1.11, instead of recopying the entire section as in VatS 15. The text of verse 11 is placed beneath the text of verse 5 in ModE M.1.11, instead of recopying the entire section as in VatS 15. The opening initial has been torn out in ModE M.1.11, and the opening intonation as well as m. 18, beat 1 through m. 21, beat 1 of S are missing. The corresponding section in ModE M.1.12 is missing, so the setting in the Modena choirbooks contains only the odd-numbered verses.

Musical structure

Verse	Music
1. Anima mea	A
2. Et exsultavit	B
3. Quia respexit	C
4. Quia fecit	D
5. Et misericordia	E
6. Fecit potentiam	B
7. Deposuit	F
8. Esurientes	G
9. Suscepit Israel	C
10. Sicut locutus	D
11. Gloria Patri	E
12. Sicut erat	F

Notes. M. 2, T, note 4 to m. 3, note 1, minim e', minim e', amended as in ModE M.1.11. M. 6, T, note 2, d' in VatS 15. M. 50, S, notes 1–2, breves in VatS 15; amended as in ModE M.1.11. M. 61, T, note 2, d' in VatS 15.

Variants in ModE M.1.11. M. 1, B, labeled "Contra." M. 2, T, note 4 to m. 3, note 1, semibreve e'. M. 50, S, notes 1–2, minim c", minim d". M. 74, S, note 3 to m. 75, note 2, not minor color. M. 80, S, notes 3–4, not minor color.

15. Magnificat 3. toni (2)

Primary source. VerBC 759, fols. 73v–75r.

Concordant sources. MunBS 3154, fols. 121r–122v, Jo. Martini 3cundi [sic] toni. MilD 1, fols. 23v–27r.

Modern editions. Brawley, 2:40–51. Noblitt, 81:101–8. Gerber, 14–19. AMMM, 12:98.

Text source. See no. 13 above.

Text. See no. 13 above.

Comment. Alternatim setting, only the odd-numbered verses are set as polyphony.

Notes. M. 69, T, note 1 to m. 70, note 1, dotted long; this is a mistake, and the other sources vary at this point. M. 113, A, note 1, an extra minim rest after this note. M. 117, A, note 2, missing breve; amended as in the concordances. M. 170, T, note 1, B; changed to A as in the concordances. M. 184, A, note 4 to m. 185, note 2, original reading creates parallel fifths; amended as in the concordances. M. 196, T, notes 1–4, missing; the reconstruction is based on MunBS 3154.

Variants. Intonation, notes 1–3, g, a, g, c′ in MilD 1. Intonation, missing in MunBS 3154. M. 1, B, note 1 to m. 2, note 1, no ligature in MilD 1. M. 3, S, notes 1–2, semibreve g′ in MilD 1. M. 4, A, notes 1–2, dotted minim f′, semiminim e′ in MilD 1. M. 4, T, notes 3–5, ligature in MunBS 3154. M. 5, T, notes 1–2, no ligature in MunBS 3154. M. 17, S, note 3, a′ in MilD 1; this is a mistake. M. 22, A, note 3 to m. 23, note 2, minor color in MilD 1. M. 26, A, note 1 to m. 27, note 1, no ligature in MilD 1 and MunBS 3154. M. 26, S, notes 2–3, minims in MilD 1 and MunBS 3154. M. 28, A, note 3 to m. 29, note 1, no ligature in MilD 1. M. 31, S, note 2 to m. 32, note 2, d′ semiminim, e′ semiminim, f′ semiminim, g′ semiminim, a′ dotted minim, g′ semiminim in MilD 1. M. 34, B, notes 1–2, ligature in MunBS 3154. M. 36, B, notes 1–2, ligature in MunBS 3154. M. 38, A, notes 2–3, dotted minim g′, semiminim f′, semiminim d′, semiminim d′ in MunBS 3154. M. 39, B, note 1 to m. 43, note 1, ligature in MunBS 3154. M. 39, A, note 4 to m. 40, note 2, minor color in MunBS 3154. M. 43, A, notes 1–2, ligature in MilD 1 and MunBS 3154. M. 45, A, notes 1–2, ligature in MilD 1 and MunBS 3154. M. 46, B, notes 1–2, no ligature in MilD 1 and MunBS 3154. M. 47, S, note 3 to m. 48, note 2, semibreve c″, minim b′ in MilD 1 and MunBS 3154. M. 48, A, note 3, fusa b′, fusa a′ in MilD 1.

M. 51, B, note 3, f in MilD 1. M. 51, B, note 3 to m. 52, note 3, semiminim g, semiminim f, minim e, minim c, minim d, minim e in MunBS 3154. M. 52, T, note 1 to m. 92, note 1, this section is copied a third higher in MunBS 3154; the clef is C3 and should be C4. M. 52, A, note 1, minim a′, minim c′ in MilD 1. M. 52, A, note 1, semibreve d′, semibreve c′ in MunBS 3154. M. 52, A, notes 1–2, no ligature in MunBS 3154. M. 56, S, note 1 to m. 59, note 4, breve rest, dotted semibreve g′, minim a′, semibreve b′, minim a′, semibreve g′, semiminim f′, semiminim e′, minim d′ in MilD 1. M. 61, T, note 1 to m. 62, note 1, no ligature in MunBS 3154. M. 61, S, note 3, semiminim g′ in MunBS 3154. M. 62, B, notes 1–2, minor color in MilD 1. M. 64, T, note 1 to m. 67, note 1, ligature in MunBS 3154. M. 64, B, note 4 to m. 65, note 2, dotted minim e, semiminim f in MilD 1 and MunBS 3154. M. 66, T, note 1 to m. 69, note 1, breve c′, long c′, breve c′ in MilD 1. M. 69, S, note 6, semiminim d′ in MunBS 3154. M. 71, S, note 5 to m. 72, note 2, semibreve b′ ligated to the next note in MunBS 3154. M. 73, A, note 6 to m. 74, note 1, colored minim f′, semiminim e′ in MunBS 3154. M. 73, A, note 6 to m. 74, note 1, dotted minim f′, semiminim e′ in MilD 1. M. 75, A, notes 1–2, ligature in MilD 1 and MunBS 3154. M. 78, S, notes 2–3, minim e′ in MunBS 3154. M. 83, B, note 1, minim rest, minim G in MilD 1. M. 83, B, notes 1–2, no ligature in MilD 1. M. 83, A, note 3, semibreve b in MunBS 3154. M. 86, B, note 2, semiminim e, semiminim d in MilD 1. M. 87, A, note 2 to m. 88, note 1, no ligature in MunBS 3154. M. 89, B, note 3 to m. 90, note 1, minim a, minim a in MilD 1. M. 90, A, note 2, rest is missing in MilD 1. M. 90, S, note 3 to m. 91, note 2, minor color in MilD 1. M. 90, S, note 3 to m. 91, note 2, semibreve b′ ligated to the next note in MunBS 3154. M. 91, A, note 3 to m. 92, note 1, long e′ in MilD 1. M. 96, A, notes 1–2, no ligature in MunBS 3154. M. 99, S, note 3 to m. 100, note 1, no ligature in MilD 1.

M. 104, S, notes 1–2, no ligature in MilD 1. M. 106, S, note 2 to m. 107, note 1, ligature in MunBS 3154. M. 106, A, notes 2–3, minor color in MunBS 3154. M. 106, A, note 4 to m. 107, note 2, semibreve e′, breve d′ in MilD 1. M. 107, B, note 1 to m. 108, note 1, no ligature in MilD 1. M. 110, B, notes 1–2, no ligature in MilD 1. M. 110, S, note 3 to m. 111, note 1, semibreve g′, minim g′ in MunBS 3154. M. 110, S, note 3 to m. 111, note 2, no ligature in MunBS 3154. M. 111, T, note 1 to m. 116, note 1, no ligature in MilD 1. M. 113, S, notes 1–2, no ligature in MilD 1. M. 115, S, note 3 to m. 116, note 2, minor color in MunBS 3154. M. 115, B, note 3 to m. 116, note 2, minor color in MilD 1. M. 116, S, notes 4–6, dotted minim b′, semiminim a′ in MilD 1 and MunBS 3154. M. 117, A, note 3 to m. 118, note 2, no ligature in MilD 1. M. 118, T, note 1 to m. 119, note 1, no ligature in MilD 1. M. 120, S, notes 2–4, semiminim g′, semiminim f′, semibreve g′ in MunBS 3154. M. 120, S, notes 3–4, minim g′, semiminim f′, semiminim g′ in MilD 1. M. 124, T, note 1 to m. 129, note 1, double long a, long a in MunBS 3154. M. 124, T, note 1 to m. 129, note 1, a in MilD 1. M. 126, A, note 1 to m. 127, note 3, breve rest, semibreve a′, dotted minim a′, fusa g′, fusa f′ in MunBS 3154. M. 127, S, note 3 to m. 128, note 3, dotted minim a′, semibreve b′, dotted minim c″, semiminim b′ in MilD 1 and MunBS 3154. M. 128, B, notes 1–2, dotted semibreve A in MilD 1. M. 129, A, note 3 to m. 130, note 1, no ligature in MunBS 3154. M. 131, T, notes 1–2, ligature in MilD 1 and MunBS 3154. M. 131, B, notes 1–2, no ligature in MilD 1. M. 131, A, note 2 to m. 132, note 2, no ligature in MunBS 3154. M. 132, S, note 2 to m. 133, note 1, ligature in MilD 1.   M. 132, S, note 3 to m. 133, note 2, ligature in MunBS 3154.   M. 136, S, notes 1–2, no ligature in MilD 1 and MunBS 3154.   M. 137, A, notes 1–2, no ligature in MilD 1 and MunBS 3154.   M. 138, A, notes 1–2, no ligature in MilD 1.   M. 141, A, notes 3–4, minim a′, minim b′ in MilD 1.   M. 142, A, notes 1–2, no ligature in MilD 1.   M. 144, A, note 2, dotted minim c′, semiminim b in MunBS 3154.   M. 148, T, note 1, no ♭ in MunBS 3154.   M. 148, S, note 4, ♭ in MilD 1.

M. 150, S, note 4 to m. 151, note 2, semibreve d′ ligated to the next note in MunBS 3154.   M. 151, T, notes 1–2, ligature in MilD 1 and MunBS 3154.   M. 153, A, notes 3–4, minim e′, minim f′ in MunBS 3154.   M. 154, A, note 1 to m. 155, note 1, ligature in MilD 1.   M. 154, S, note 3 to m. 155, note 2, ligature in MunBS 3154.   M. 169, S, notes 1–2, ligature in MilD 1.   M. 171, S, notes 1–5, dotted minim f′, semiminim g′, minim a′, semiminim g′, semiminim f′ in MilD 1.   M. 171, T, notes 1–6, minim b, semiminim a, semiminim g, semibreve f in MilD 1.   M. 172, B, note 1 to m. 175, note 1, no ligature in MilD 1.   M. 172, B, note 1, no ligature in MunBS 3154.   M. 177, T, note 1, semibreve a, minim a in MilD 1.   M. 177, T, note 1 to m. 178, note 1, no ligature in MilD 1.   M. 177, B, note 1 to m. 178, note 1, no ligature in MilD 1.   M. 177, T, note 2 to m. 178, note 2, not minor color in MilD 1.   M. 179, S, note 1 to m. 180, note 1, no ligature in MilD 1.   M. 179, A, note 1, semibreve e′, minim e′ in MilD 1.   M. 179, A, note 1 to m. 180, note 1, no ligature in MilD 1 and MunBS 3154.   M. 179, T, note 1, semibreve b, minim b in MilD 1.   M. 179, T, note 1 to m. 180, note 1, no ligature in MilD 1.   M. 179, T, note 1 to m. 180, note 1, semibreve b, semibreve rest, minim c′ in MunBS 3154.   M. 179, S, note 2 to m. 180, note 2, not minor color in MilD 1.   M. 179, A, note 2 to m. 180, note 2, not minor color in MilD 1.   M. 182, S, notes 5–6, minor color in MunBS 3154.   M. 183, A, note 5 to m. 184, note 1, dotted minim e′, semiminim d′ in MunBS 3154.   M. 184, A, note 4 to m. 185, note 2, dotted minim e′, semiminim d′ in MilD 1 and MunBS 3154.   M. 185, T, note 4 to m. 186, note 1, ligature in MunBS 3154.   M. 186, A, note 3 to m. 187, note 1, ligature in MunBS 3154.   M. 187, S, notes 1–2, no ligature in MunBS 3154.   M. 189, A, note 2 to m. 190, note 1, no ligature in MilD 1.   M. 192, S, note 1 to m. 193, note 1, no ligature in MilD 1.   M. 192, A, notes 3–4, dotted minim e′, semiminim f′ in MilD 1 and MunBS 3154.   M. 193, T, note 5 to m. 194, note 2, semibreve d′ ligated to the next note in MunBS 3154.   M. 195, T, note 2 to m. 196, note 3, minim a, semibreve c′, minim d′, minim c′ in MunBS 3154.   M. 195, T, note 2 to m. 196, note 6, minim a, semibreve c′, minim d′, minim c′, semiminim b, semiminim a in MilD 1.   M. 196, S, notes 3–4, minor color in MunBS 3154.   M. 197, S, note 4 to m. 198, note 2, semibreve d″ ligated to the next note in MunBS 3154.   M. 198, A, note 3 to m. 199, note 1, ligature in MilD 1.   M. 199, A, notes 1–2, no ligature in MilD 1 and MunBS 3154.

M. 200, T, note 4, dotted minim e, semiminim d in MunBS 3154.   M. 202, S, notes 1–2, minim a′, semiminim g′, semiminim f′ in MilD 1.   M. 205, S, note 1 to m. 206, note 1, no ligature in MilD 1.   M. 205, A, note 1 to m. 206, note 1, ligature in MilD 1 and MunBS 3154.   M. 205, T, note 1 to m. 207, note 4, semibreve a ligated to semibreve c′, minim d′, minim e′, dotted minim f′, semiminim e′, semiminim d′, semiminim c′, minim d′ in MilD 1.   M. 206, A, note 4, ♭ in MilD 1 and MunBS 3154.   M. 207, S, note 6 to m. 208, note 2, semibreve b′ ligated to the next note in MunBS 3154.

16. *Magnificat 4. toni*

Primary source.   VatS 15, fols. 100v–107r.

Concordant source.   MunBS 3154, fols. 118v–120v, Io Martini.

Modern editions.   Brawley, 2:52–64. Noblitt, 81:92–100.

Text source.   See no. 13 above.

Text.   See no. 13 above.

Notes.   M. 11, A, note 4, semibreve d; amended to a breve as in MunBS 3154.

Variants in MunBS 3154.   M. 5, S, note 2, g′.   M. 8, S, notes 3–4, not minor color.   M. 9, S, note 5 to m. 10, note 2, breve a′ ligated to the next note.   M. 12, S, notes 2–4, dotted semibreve g′, minim f′, semibreve e′.   M. 13, A, notes 2–3, not minor color.   M. 15, A, note 1, upper note colored.   Mm. 16–38, B, 27 rests; there should be 23.   M. 22, T, notes 1–2, not minor color.   M. 29, S, notes 3–4, not minor color.   M. 44, A, note 4 to m. 45, note 2, not minor color.   M. 58, A, notes 1–2, no ligature.   M. 60, B, note 1 to m. 62, note 1, ligature.   M. 62, A, note 1 to m. 63, note 1, ligature. M. 70, A, note 1 to m. 71, note 1, ligature.   M. 71, B, notes 1–2, no ligature.   M. 74, A, note 1 to m. 75, note 1, ligature.   M. 86, S, note 4 to m. 87, note 2, semibreve f′ ligated to the next note.   M. 86, A, note 5, d′.   M. 91, S, note 6 to m. 92, note 2, semibreve a′ ligated to the next note.   M. 91, B, note 4 to m. 92, note 2, not minor color.   M. 93, A, notes 2–3, not minor color. M. 93, S, note 3 to m. 94, note 2, not minor color.   M. 94, A, note 4 to m. 95, note 2, ligature.

M. 100, T, notes 1–2, ligature.   M. 102, S, note 3, d′. M. 106, B, notes 2–3, ligature.   M. 107, S, notes 2–3, not minor color.   M. 107, T, notes 1–2, ligature.   M. 107, T, notes 2–3, no ligature.   M. 108, T, notes 2–3, not minor color.   M. 109, A, note 1 to m. 110, note 3, semibreve d′, minim b, semibreve e′, minim c′, semibreve d′, minim b, semibreve e′, minim d′, semibreve e′; there are several mistakes here: the first two notes are extra, and the seventh should be dotted. M. 109, T, notes 2–3, not minor color. M. 109, T, notes 5–6, not minor color. M. 110, S, note 2, f′. M. 110, T, notes 2–3, not minor color. M. 113, T, notes 4–5, not minor color. M. 114, S, notes 3–4, ligature. M. 115, A, notes 1–2, not minor color. M. 122, A, note 1 to m. 123, note 1, no ligature. M. 124, T, note 2, c. M. 124, T, notes 1–2, no ligature. M. 132, T, note 4 to m. 133, note 2, semibreve a ligated to the next note. M. 134, T, notes 1–2, no ligature. M. 136, T, notes 2–4, dotted minim d, fusa c, fusa d. M. 143, A, note 2 to m. 144, note 1, dotted semibreve a. M. 156, T, note 2 to m. 157, note 1, no ligature. M. 156, T, notes 1–2, ligature. M. 161, S, notes 3–4, dotted minim f′, semiminim e′. M. 162, A, note 3 to m. 163, note 1, minim b, minim c′, long b. M. 167, A, note 3, dotted minim b, semiminim a. M. 179, S, note 1 to m. 180, note 1, ligature. M. 179, B, note 1 to m. 180, note 1, ligature. M. 183, A, notes 2–3, semibreve g. M. 194, T, note 1 to m. 195, note 1, ligature.

M. 204, S, note 1 to m. 205, note 1, no ligature. M. 205, B, note 1, no ligature. M. 205, B, notes 1–3, not minor color. M. 206, B, note 1 to m. 208, note 1, ligature. M. 211, S, note 1 to m. 212, note 1, no ligature. M. 212, A, note 3, dotted minim b, semiminim a. M. 213, A, note 2, rest is missing. M. 214, T, note 1 to m. 217, note 1, double long.

17. *Magnificat 6. toni*

Primary source. VatS 15, fols. 134v–140r.

Concordant source. MunBS 3154, 123v–125r, Io Martini.

Modern editions. Brawley, 2: 65–76. Noblitt, 81:109–17.

Text source. See no. 13 above.

Text. See no. 13 above.

Notes. M. 57, note 2, T, d in VatS 15; this is a mistake, amended as in MunBS 3154. M. 71, B, notes 3–4, notated as minims in VatS 15; amended as in MunBS 3154. M. 91, T, note 3, d′ in VatS 15; amended as in MunBS 3154. M. 289, T, note 2, d in VatS 15; amended as in MunBS 3154. M. 368, A, notes 1–4, semibreve a′, minim g′, minim f′, semibreve e′; this reading creates parallel fifths, amended as in m. 177.

Variants in MunBS 3154. M. 6, S, note 1, minim g′, minim g′. M. 7, B, note 4, ♭. M. 13, A, notes 2–3, minor color. M. 16, T, notes 2–3, minor color. M. 20, T, notes 1–2, semibreve e′, semibreve e′. M. 21, S, note 2 to m. 22, note 2, semibreve g′, semibreve g′. M. 25, A, notes 2–3, not minor color. M. 25, T, notes 2–3, not minor color. M. 29, S, note 2 to m. 30, note 2, ligature. M. 29, A, notes 2–3, not minor color. M. 37, S, note 2 to m. 38, note 1, minim c″, minim c″, minim c″. M. 38, A, note 1 to m. 39, note 1, ligature. M. 38, T, note 2, minim e′, minim e′. M. 40, S, notes 1–2, not minor color. M. 40, B, note 3, minim f, minim f. M. 43, S, note 5 to m. 44, note 6, semibreve d″ ligated to semibreve c″, minim b′. M. 44, A, note 3 to m. 45, note 1, semibreve g′, long g′. M. 47, S, notes 2–3, minim b′. M. 48, T, notes 2–3, ligature. M. 49, S, notes 1–2, perfect breve c″. M. 50, A, notes 3–6, semibreve g′, minim f′. M. 51, T, notes 1–2, breve d′. M. 51, B, notes 2–3, not minor color. M. 53, T, note 1 to m. 54, note 1, colored breve e′, colored breve e′, colored breve e′. M. 54, S, notes 1–2, semibreve b′, dotted semibreve e″. M. 57, S, notes 4–7, semibreve c″, minim b′. M. 59, T, note 3 to m. 60, note 2, not minor color. M. 61, T, note 1, no fermata. M. 62, B, notes 3–4, not minor color. M. 67, B, notes 2–3, minor color. M. 67, B, notes 4–5, minor color. M. 71, A, notes 1–2, minor color. M. 71, A, notes 4–5, minor color. M. 71, B, note 5 to m. 72, note 1, ligature. M. 78, S, notes 1–2, minor color. M. 78, S, notes 5–8, semibreve c″, minim b′. M. 78, B, notes 1–2, not minor color. Mm. 80–112, missing.

M. 113, S, note 1, rest is missing. M. 116, A, notes 3–4, missing. M. 117, S, notes 1–2, missing. M. 125, S, note 2 to m. 126, note 1, ligature. M. 130, S, note 5 to m. 131, note 2, semibreve a′ (ligated to the next g′). M. 141, S, notes 2–4, minim d″, semiminim c″, semiminim b′. M. 144, S, note 5 to m. 145, note 2, not minor color. M. 147, A, note 1, breve rest. M. 149, A, note 1 to m. 150, note 1, ligature. M. 155, T, note 1, breve c′, semibreve c′. M. 157, T, note 1, breve e′, semibreve e′. M. 166, T, note 1 to m. 167, note 1, ligature. M. 167, B, note 1 to m. 168, note 3, colored. M. 170, B, note 12, ♭. M. 173, A, note 1 to m. 174, note 1, ligature. M. 181, T, note 1 to m. 182, note 1, no ligature. M. 182, B, notes 1–2, ligature. M. 185, T, note 1, missing. M. 188, T, note 1, breve c′, semibreve c′. M. 189, T, note 2, semibreve f′, semibreve f′. M. 192, A, notes 1–2, ligature. M. 200, S, notes 2–3, colored. M. 200, A, note 2, no ♭. M. 201, S, note 2, not colored. M. 202, A, note 1, ♭. M. 203, S, notes 1–2, ligature. M. 203, A, note 1, minim a′; this is a mistake. M. 203, A, notes 1–2, ligature. M. 204, S, notes 1–4, breve c″, semibreve b′. Mm. 206–432, missing.

18. *Magnificat 6. toni (Johannes Brebis)*

Primary source. ModE M.1.11, fols. 39v–41r, Brebis.

Text source. See no. 13 above.

Text. See no. 13 above.

Comment. The corresponding section of ModE M.1.12 is missing; so this setting uses only the odd-numbered verses.

Note. M. 34, A, note 2, semibreve.

19. Magnificat 8. toni (1)

Primary source. MunBS 3154, fols. 124v–126r, Jo. Martini.

Modern editions. Brawley, 2:77–79. Noblitt, 81:118–19.

Text source. See no. 13 above.

Text. See no. 13 above.

Comment. This piece is fragmentary; all that survives is a setting of the first two stanzas and the S and A of the third. These last two voices are not a stand-alone duet and are not included here.

Note. M. 27, A, note 5, semibreve d′, minim d′; the extra minim is a mistake.

20. Magnificat 8. toni (2)

Primary source. MilD 1, fols. 27v–29r, Jo. Martini.

Concordant source. VerBC 758, fols. 113v–115r.

Modern editions. Brawley, 2:80–87. *AMMM*, 12:1–6.

Text source. See no. 13 above.

Text. See no. 13 above.

Comment. Alternatim setting, only the odd-numbered verses are set as polyphony.

Notes. Intonation, an extra c, amended as in VerBC 758. M. 21, A, note 3, fermata, which indicates the entrance of the B after a long rest. M. 33, B, note 2 to m. 34, note 1, minim g, minim f, semibreve g; this creates an unusual dissonance with the S; amended as in VerBC 758. M. 35, B, note 1 to m. 37, note 2, minim rest, minim d, minim f, minim c, semibreve g, minim d, semibreve f, minim g; this reading creates unusual dissonances with both the S and A; amended as in VerBC 758. M. 121, B, note 1, f; this is a mistake, amended as in VerBC 758. M. 137, A, note 2, f′; this is a mistake, amended as in VerBC 758.

Variants in VerBC 758. M. 1, S, note 1, dotted semibreve c″. M. 2, T, note 1, dotted semibreve c′. M. 3, S, notes 2–3, minim rest, semibreve c″, semiminim b′, semiminim a′. M. 4, S, notes 2–3, not minor color. M. 8, B, note 1, long g only. M. 11, A, notes 1–2, no ligature. M. 11, A, note 2 to m. 12, note 1, ligature. M. 12, S, notes 1–2, no ligature. M. 12, A, note 1 to m. 13, note 1, no ligature. M. 13, S, note 1 to m. 14, note 1, no ligature. M. 16, A, note 1, no ♭. M. 17, S, note 1, no ♭. M. 17, S, notes 1–3, dotted minim b′, fusa a′, fusa g′. M. 24, A, note 4 to m. 25, note 2, not minor color. M. 26, B, note 2, semibreve d. M. 26, B, notes 1–2, ligature. M. 33, B, note 2 to m. 34, note 1, semibreve g, minim f, minim g. M. 35, B, note 1 to m. 37, note 2, breve rest, minim d, minim f, minim d, semibreve g, minim c. M. 36, S, note 5, no ♭. M. 36, A, note 3 to m. 37, note 2, minim c′, minim d′, minim b. M. 41, B, note 1 to m. 42, note 1, no ligature. M. 43, S, note 1 to m. 44, note 1, no ligature. M. 45, T, note 1 to m. 46, note 1, no ligature. M. 47, S, notes 1–2, no ligature. M. 47, T, note 1 to m. 48, note 1, no ligature. M. 47, B, note 1 to m. 50, note 1, ligature. M. 49, T, note 1 to m. 50, note 1, no ligature. M. 55, A, note 3, semiminim a′, semiminim g′. M. 59, S, notes 1–2, no ligature. M. 65, A, note 3, long d′. M. 66, B, note 1, long g. M. 69, S, note 1 to m. 70, note 1, breve g′, semibreve g′. M. 70, S, notes 1–2, ligature. M. 71, A, note 1 to m. 72, note 2, breve g, semibreve g. M. 72, A, notes 1–2, ligature. M. 89, S, note 1 to m. 90, note 1, no ligature. M. 91, A, note 1 to m. 92, note 1, no ligature. M. 93, S, note 5 to m. 94, note 2, not minor color. M. 96, S, note 1 to m. 97, note 1, no ligature. M. 97, S, note 2 to m. 98, note 2, no ligature. M. 97, A, notes 1–2, no ligature. M. 98, A, notes 1–2, no ligature.

M. 101, A, note 3 to m. 102, note 4, semiminim g′, semiminim f′, semiminim e′; this is a mistake. M. 111, A, note 2 to m. 113, note 5, minim f′, semibreve g′, semibreve a′, breve f′. M. 112, S, note 1 to m. 113, note 5, semibreve b′, semibreve c″, breve a, all ligated. M. 114, B, note 2 to m. 116, note 5, minim f, semibreve g, semibreve a, breve f. M. 115, T, note 1 to m. 117, note 5, semibreve b, semibreve c′, breve a, all ligated. M. 117, S, notes 1–2, no ligature. M. 118, S, note 2 to m. 120, note 1, no ligature. M. 120, A, note 3 to m. 122, note 1, no ligature. M. 121, S, note 1 to m. 122, note 1, no ligature. M. 122, T, notes 1–2, ligated separately. M. 122, B, note 1 to m. 123, note 1, no ligature. M. 123, T, note 1 to m. 124, note 1, ligated separately. M. 125, T, note 1 to m. 127, note 1, ligated separately. M. 126, A, note 2 to m. 128, note 1, no ligature. M. 127, T, notes 1–2, ligature. M. 129, S, note 3 to m. 130, note 2, dotted semibreve c″, minim b′, minim b′, minim a′. M. 129, B, note 1 to m. 130, note 1, ligature. M. 131, A, notes 1–2, no ligature. M. 131, B, note 1 to m. 132, note 1, no ligature. M. 133, A, note 1 to m. 134, note 1, no ligature. M. 137, A, note 2, semibreve g′. M. 137, A, notes 1–2, no ligature. M. 138, A, note 2 to m. 139, note 1, minim g′, minim b′ M. 139, A, note 1, no ♭. M. 140, S, note 2, no ♭.

21. Magnificat 8. toni (3)

Primary source. ModE M.1.11, fol. 39r.

Text source. See no. 13 above.

Text. See no. 13 above.

Comment. The corresponding section of ModE M.1.12 is missing; so this setting uses only the odd-numbered verses.

22. *Ave decus virginale*

Primary source. 1503[1], fols. 62v–63r, Jo Marti.

Use. Verses 7–8 of the Marian sequence "Ave, virgo gratiosa."

Modern editions. Brawley, 2:52–64. DrakePM, 2:273–75. DrakeMRM, 270–72.

Text source. AH, 54:419–20.

Text

Ave decus virginale,
Templum Dei speciale,
Per te fiat veniale
Omne quod committimus.
Tu nobis es singularis,
Tu nos ducas, stella maris,
Tu nos semper tuearis,
En, ad te confugimus.

* * *

Hail, virginal honor,
individual temple of God,
through you may all the sins
that we commit be pardoned.
You are remarkable to us,
may you lead us, star of the sea,
may you always watch over us,
behold, we take refuge in you.

23. *Da pacem, Domine*

Primary source. DresSL 1/D/505, pp. 434–35, Johannes Martini.

Use. Benediction for peace.

Rubric. "Tenor altus fuga."

Text source. LU, 1867.

Text

Da pacem, Domine, in diebus nostris;
quia non est alius, quia pugnet pro nobis,
nisi tu, Deus noster.

* * *

Give us peace, O Lord, in our time;
for there is no one else who would fight for us,
except you, our Lord.

24. *Domine, non secundum*

Primary source. ModE M.1.11, fols. 46v–49r, Io Martini.

Use. Tract for the mass on Mondays, Wednesdays, and Fridays from Ash Wednesday to Wednesday of Holy Week.

Modern edition. Brawley, 2:116–22.

Text source. LU, 527. Graduale Romanum, 64.

Text

Domine, non secundum peccata nostra, que fecimus nos:
Neque secundum iniquitates nostras retribuas nobis.
Domine, ne memineris iniquitatum nostrarum antiquarum:
Cito anticipent nos misericordie tue,
Quia pauperes facti sumus nimis.
Adjuva nos, Deus salutaris noster.
Et propter gloriam nominis tui, Domine, libera nos.
Et propitius esto peccatis nostris, propter nomen tuum.

* * *

Lord, do not punish us according to our sins that we have committed:
nor according to our wickedness.
Lord, do not remember our past transgressions:
may they anticipate your mercy soon,
since we have become exceedingly wretched.
Help us, God our salvation:
and through the honor of your name, Lord, free us
and be favorably disposed to our sins, for the sake of your name.

25. *Levate capita vestra*

Primary source. 1505[2], S, fols. 15r–15v, Jo. Martini; T, fols. 46r–46v; A, fol. 78v; B, fols. 111r–111v.

Use. Antiphon for first vespers on Christmas Day.

Modern editions. Sherr, 89–102. Brawley, 2:123–32.

Text source. The text is cobbled together from various chants of first vespers for Christmas Day. Line 1 is taken from antiphon 5. Line 2 is taken from the first half of antiphon 4. Line 3 is taken from Psalm 75 (76), verse 2. Line 4 is taken from the second half of antiphon 4. Line 6 is taken from the antiphon to the Magnificat. Line 7 is taken from the verse and responsory. Line 8 is taken from antiphon 1.

Text

Levate capita vestra: ecce appropinquat redemptio vestra. Alleluya.
Scitote quia prope est regnum Dei.
Magnum nomen ejus. Emanuel. Alleluya.
Amen dico vobis, quia non tardabit. Alleluya.
Exultemus et letemur et reddamus gloriam ei. Alleluya.
Cum ortus fuerit sol de celo, videbitis Regem regum procedentem a Patre, tamquam sponsum de thalamo suo.

Crastina die delebitur iniquitas terre. Et regnabit super nos Salvator Mundi. Alleluya.

Rex pacificus, Salvator noster, magnificatus est, cujus vultum desiderat universa terra. Alleluya.

* * *

Lift up your heads: behold, your redemption approaches. Alleluya.

Know that the kingdom of God is near.

His name is great. Emanuel. Alleluya.

Truly, I say to you that it will not be delayed. Alleluya.

Let us rejoice and be glad and restore his glory.

When the sun has risen in the heavens, you will see the kind of kings come forth from the Father as a bridegroom from his bedroom.

Tomorrow the inequity of the world will be destroyed. And the savior of the world will reign over us.

The Peaceful King, our Savior, is exalted, the whole world desires to see his face. Alleluya.

Note. M. 134, S, "vos" instead of "nos."

26. *O beate Sebastiane*

Primary source. 1505[2], S, fol. 16r, Jo. Martini; T, fols. 46v–47r; A, fols. 79r–79v; B, fol. 112r.

Concordant source. BarcBC 454, [xiv verso]–xvi, Jo. Moton. Fragmentary; fol. xiv is missing, and the piece is missing the S and T for the first section of the motet.

Use. Motet for the feast of Sebastiani (20 January).

Modern editions. Brawley, 2:133–39. Ros-Fábregas, 2:43–52. Sherr, 103–11.

Text source. Unknown.

Text

O beate Sebastiane.

Miles beastissime cujus precibus tota patria lombardie fuit liberata a pestifera peste.

Libera nos ab ipsa et a maligno ut digni efficiamur promissionibus Christi.

* * *

O blessed Sebastiane.

Most holy soldier, whose prayers freed all of Lombardia from the deadly plague.

Free us from this and from evil so that we might be made worthy of the promises of Christ.

Note. M. 140, S, note 4, g' in both sources.

Variants in BarcBC 454. M. 15, A, note 1, no fermata. M. 16, A, note 1, fermata. M. 16, B, note 1, fermata. M. 63, A, note 1, no ♭. M. 74, S, "Secunda pars." M. 93, B, note 3, no ♭. M. 101, A, notes 3–4, rhythm is semibreve, minim. M. 101, B, notes 3–4, rhythm is semibreve, minim. M. 103, B, note 1, no ♭. M. 129, B, note 1, no ♭.

27. *Jesum Nazarenum*

Primary source. ModE M.1.12, fols. 97v–101r.

Use. Easter passion.

Text source. John 18–19 (selections).

Text

[Turba]: Jesum Nazarenum. [18:5]

Ancilla: Numquid et tu ex discipulis es hominis istius? [18:17]

Petrus: Non sum. [18:17]

[Unus assistens]: Sic respondes pontifici? [18:22]

[Turba]: Numquid et tu ex discipulis ejus es? [18:25]

Petrus: Non sum. [18:25]

Servus pontificis: Nonne ego te vidi in orto cum illo? [18:26]

Pilatus: Quam accusationem affertis adversus hominem hunc? [18:29]

[Turba]: Si non esset hic malefactor, non tibi tradidissemus eum. [18:30]

Pilatus: Accipite eum vos, et secundum legem vestram judicate eum. [18:31]

[Judei]: Nobis non licet interficere quemquam. [18:31]

Pilatus: Tu es rex Judeorum? [18:33]

Pilatus: Numquid ego Judeus sum? Gens tua et pontifices tua tradiderunt te michi: quid fecisti? [18:35]

Pilatus: Ergo rex es tu? [18:37]

Pilatus: Quid es veritas? [18:38]

Pilatus: Ego nullam causam invenio in eo. Est autem consuetudo vobis in Pascha, ut unum dimittam vultis ut dimittam vobis regem Judeorum? [18:38–39]

[Turba]: Non hunc, sed Barabam [18:40]

[Milites]: Ave rex Judeorum. [19:3]

Pilatus: Ecce adduco eum vobis foras, ut cognoscatis quia in eo nullam causa invenio. [19:4]

Pilatus: Ecce homo. [19:5]

[Pontifices et ministri]: Crucifige, crucifige eum. [19:6]

Pilatus: Accipite eum vos, et crucifigite; ego enim non invenio in eo causam. [19:6]

[Judei]: Nos legem habemus, et secundum legem nostram debet mori quia filium Dei se fecit. [19:7]

Pilatus: Unde es tu? [19:9]

Pilatus: Michi non loqueris? Nescis quia potestatem habeo crucifigere te, et potestatem habeo dimittere te? [19:10]

[Judei]: Si hunc dimittis, non eris amicus Cesaris. Omnis enim qui se regem facit, contradicit Cesari. [19:12]

Pilatus: Ecce rex vester. [19:14]

[Judei]: Tolle, tolle, crucifige eum. [19:15]

Pilatus: Regem vestrum crucifigam? [19:15]
[Judei]: Non habemus regem, nisi Cesarem. [19:15]
[Pontifices Judeorum]: Noli scribere: Rex Judeorum: sed quia ipse dixit: sum Rex Judeorum. [19:21]
Pilatus: Quod scripsi, scripsi. [19:22]
[Milites]: Non scindamus eam sed sortiamur de illa cujus sit. [19:24]

* * *

[Crowd]: Jesus of Nazareth.
Woman: Are not thou also one of this man's disciples?
Peter: I am not.
[Servant]: Answerest thou the high priest so?
[Crowd]: Art not thou also one of his disciples?
Peter: I am not.
Servant of the high priest: Did not I see thee in the garden with him?
Pilate: What accusation do you bring against this man?
Crowd: If he were not a malefactor, we would not have delivered him up to thee.
Pilate: Take him, and judge him according to your law.
Jews: It is not lawful for us to put any man to death.
Pilate: Art thou the king of the Jews?
Pilate: Am I a Jew? Thy own nation, and the chief priests have delivered thee up to my: what hast thou done?
Pilate: Art thou a king then?
Pilate: What is truth?
Pilate: I find no cause in him. But you have a custom that I should release one unto you at the Pasch: will you, therefore, that I release unto you the king of the Jews?
[Crowd]: Not this man, but Barabas.
[Soldiers]: Hail, king of the Jews.
Pilate: Behold, I bring him forth unto you, that you may know that I find no cause in him.
Pilate: Behold the man.
[Priests and servants]: Crucify him, crucify him.
Pilate: Take him, and crucify him, for I find no cause in him.
[Jews]: We have a law; and according to our law he ought to die, because he made himself the Son of God.
Pilate: Whence art thou?
Pilate: Speakest thou not to me? Knowest thou not that I have the power to crucify thee, and I have the power to release thee?
[Jews]: If thou release this man, thou art not Cesar's friend. For whosoever maketh himself a King, speaketh against Cesar.
Pilate: Behold your king.
[Jews]: Away with him, away with him, crucify him.

Pilate: Shall I crucify your king?
[Jews]: We have no king but Cesar.
[Chief Priest]: Write not, the King of the Jews, but that he said, I am king of the Jews.
Pilate: What I have written, I have written.
[Soldiers]: Let us not cut it, but let us cast lots for it, whose it shall be.

Comment. The following character parts appear on the top staff in order of appearance: Turba 1, Ancilla, Servus pontificis, Judei 1, Milites 1, Pontifices et ministri 1, Pontifices Judeorum 1. The following character parts appear on the bottom staff in order of appearance: Turba 2, Petrus, Unus assistens, Pilatus, Judei 2, Milites 2, Pontifices et ministri 2, Pontifices Judeorum 2.

Notes. M. 119, S, note 1, not colored. Mm. 265–66, S, "Rex sum." M. 271, S, note 2, semibreve. Mm. 286–87, B, "ea."

28. *Non in die festo*

Primary source. ModE M.1.12, fols. 91v–97r.

Use. Easter passion.

Text source. Matthew 26–27 (selections).

Text

[Principes sacerdotem]: Non in die festo, ne forte tumultus fieret in populo. [26:5]
[Discipuli]: Ut quid perditio hec? Poterat enim unguentum istud venundari multo, et dari pauperibus. [26:9]
Judas: Quid vultis michi dare, et ego eum vobis tradam. [26:15]
[Discipuli]: Ubi vis paremus tibi commedere pascha? [26:17]
[Discipuli]: Numquid ego sum Domine? [26:22]
Judas: Numquid ego sum rabi? [26:25]
Petrus: Et si omnes scandalizati fuerint in te, ego numquam scandalizabor. [26:33]
Petrus: Etiamsi oportuerit me mori tecum, non te negabo. [26:35]
Judas: Quemcumque osculatus fuero, ipse est, tenete eum. [26:48]
Judas: Ave rabi. [26:49]
[Falsi testi]: Hic dicit: Possum destruere templum Dei, et post triduum rehedificare illud. [26:61]
Annas: Nichil respondes ad ea que isti adversum te testificantur? [26:62]
Annas: Adjuro te per Deum vivum, ut dicas nobis si tu es Christus filius Dei. [26:63]
Annas: Blasfemavit: quid adhuc egemus testibus? Ecce nunc audistis blasfemiam quid vobis videtur? [26:65–66]

[Falsi testi]: Reus est mortis. [26:66]
[Annas]: Prophetiza nobis Christe, quis est qui te percussit? [26:68]
Prima ancilla: Et tu cum Jesu Nazareno eras. [26:69]
Petrus: Nescio quid dicis. [26:70]
Secunda ancilla: Et hic erat cum Jesu Nazareno. [26:71]
Judei: Vere [et] tu ex illis es: Nam et loquella tua manifestum te facit. [26:73]
Judas: Peccavi tradens sanguinem justum. [27:4]
Judei: Quid ad nos? Tu videris. [27:4]
[Annas]: Non licet eos mittere in corbonam: quia pretium sanguinis est. [27:6]
Pilatus: Tu es rex judeorum? [27:11]
Pilatus: Non audis quanta adversum te dicunt testimonia. [27:13]
Pilatus: Quem vultis dimittam vobis: Barabam, an Jesum, qui dicitur Christus? [27:17]
Uxor Pilatus: Nichil tibi, et justo illi: multa enim hodie passa sunt per visum propter eum. [27:19]
Pilatus: Quem vultis vobis de duobus dimitti? [27:21]
[Judei]: Barabam. [27:21]
Pilatus: Quid igitur faciam de Jesu qui dicitur Christus. [27:22]
[Judei]: Crucifigatur. [27:23]
Pilatus: Quid enim mali fecit? [27:23]
[Judei]: Crucifigatur. [27:23]
Pilatus: Innocens ego sum a sanguine justi hujus: vos videritis. [27:24]
Judei: Sanguis ejus super nos, et super filios nostros. [27:25]
Judas: Ave rex Judeorum. [27:29]
Judei: Vath qui destruis templum Dei, et post triduum illud rehedificas salva te ipsum: si filius Dei es, descende de cruce. [27:40]
Judei: Alios salvos fecit, seipsum salvum facere non potest: si rex Israel est, descendet de cruce et credimus ei: confidit in Deum liberet eum si vult, dixit enim: quia filius dei sum. [27:42–43]
Judei: Heliam vocat iste. [27:47]
[Judei]: Sine videamus an veniat Helias liberans eum. [27:49]
[Centurio]: Vere filius dei erat iste. [27:54]

* * *

[Chief priests]: Not on the festival day, lest perhaps there should be a tumult among the people.
[Disciples]: To what purpose is this waste? For this might have been sold for much, and given to the poor.
Judas: What will you give me, and I will deliver him to you?
[Disciples]: Where would you have us prepare for you to eat the pasch?
[Disciples]: Is it I, Lord?
Judas: Is it I, Rabbi?
Peter: And even if all are scandalized in you, I will never be scandalized.
Peter: Even if I were to die with you, I will not deny you.
Judas: Whomsoever I shall kiss, that is he, hold him.
Judas: Hail Rabbi.
[False witnesses]: This man said: I can destroy the temple of God, and after three days rebuild it.
Annas [High Priest]: Do you answer nothing to what these [witnesses] testify against you?
Annas: I implore you by the living God, tell us if you are Christ the son of God.
Annas: He has blasphemed. For what do we still need witnesses? Behold, now you have heard the blasphemy, what does he seem to you?
[False witnesses]: The defendant is dead [guilty of death].
[Annas]: Prophesy to us, Christ, who is it that struck you?
First woman: You also were with Jesus of Nazareth.
Peter: I don't know what you're talking about.
Second woman: And this man was with Jesus of Nazareth.
Jews: And surely you are one of them; for even your speech makes it manifest.
Judas: I have sinned by betraying innocent blood.
Jews: What is that to us? Look you to it.
[Annas]: It is not legal to put them in the corbona, because it is the price of blood.
Pilate: Are you king of the Jews?
Pilate: Don't you hear how great testimonies they allege against you?
Pilate: Whom do you wish that I release to you: Barabas, or Jesus, who is called Christ?
Wife of Pilate: Have nothing to do with that just man; for I have suffered many things today in a dream because of him.
Pilate: Which of the two do you want to be released to you?
[Jews]: Barabas.
Pilate: What shall I do then with Jesus who is called Christ?
[Jews]: Let him be crucified.
Pilate: What evil hath he done?
[Jews]: Let him be crucified.
Pilate: I am innocent of the blood of this just man. Look you to it.
Jews: His blood be upon us and upon our children.
Judas: Hail, king of the Jews.
Jews: Vah, who destroys the temple of God, and after three days rebuilds it: save yourself. If you are the son of God, descend from the cross.
Jews: He saved others, himself he cannot save. If he is the king of Israel, let him descend from the cross and we will believe him. He trusted in God, let

him free him if he wants, for he said, I am the son of God.
Jews: This man calls to Elias.
[Jews]: Let him be. Let's see whether Elias will come to free him.
[Roman Centurion]: Truly this was the son of God.

Comments. In Matthew's Gospel, the high priest is Caiphas, Annas's son-in-law. The composer (or scribe) most likely knew that the two high priests were Annas and Caiphas, but took the name Annas from another account, possibly John. Similarly, the composer labeled the two false witnesses as "Populus Judeorum" (which in later passions became the turba). For the sake of clarity, I have labeled the false witnesses as "Falsi testi." The real "Populus Judeorum" are labeled simply as "Judei" in the score, and I have kept this name.

29. Perfunde celi rore

Primary source. TrentC 91, fols. 40v–42r.

Attributions. Stephan, 65, n. 28. *AMMM,* 12. Lockwood, 258.

Use. Motet for the marriage of Ercole I d'Este and Eleonora d'Aragona in 1473.

Modern edition. AMMM, 12:89–97.

Text source. Newly written.

Text

Prima pars
Perfunde celi rore
Benedic quam nuptias,
Reginam sancto more:
Ne des indutias,
Herculem servare
Per flamen spiritus.
Per terram atque mare,
Sit sibi servitus.

Secunda pars
A Virgine qui natus
Et verbum verum es,
Tu adorandus datus,
O quam miranda res,
Matrem tu creares,
Que generaret te:
In Heva commendares
Hec genuit sine ve.
Nunc tu sancte infans,
Aures aperi
Sponse que est constans;
Da gratiam Herculi,
Sponse benignitatem:
Ut ambo timeant te:
Da meram dignitatem,
Confirma hos in spe.

* * *

Prima pars
Sprinkle her with heaven's dew
bless this queen on her nuptials,
according to sacred custom:
do not cease
to preserve Ercole
through the breath of the Spirit.
Through land and sea
let him be subject to you.

Secunda pars
You are He who was born of a virgin
and are the true word,
you are the gift to be adored,
O how wonderful a thing,
you created the mother
that bore you:
this woman bore
without the woe you rendered upon Eve.
Now, you holy infant,
open the ears
of the bride who is steadfast;
grant grace to Ercole
[and] to the benevolent bride
in order that both may fear you:
give [them] pure dignity,
strengthen them in hope.

Notes. M. 18, T, the entire measure is missing in the original; probably a haplographic mistake by the scribe. M. 66, B, note 2, D; this is a mistake. M. 131, S, note 1, "es" instead of "est."

30. Hercules omni memorandus evo (Johannes Brebis)

Primary source. ModE X.1.11, fols. 76v–78r, Brebis.

Text source. Newly written. The text was edited and translated by Leofranc Holford-Strevens.

Text

Prima pars
Hercules omni memorandus evo
Hercules toto celebrandus orbe
Stirpis estensis generosa proles
   nobilis heros,
Imperi tandem cupiens habenas
Premium tanti recepit laboris
Heu quibus fatis agitata virtus
   leta quiescit.
Herculis digna est probitas honore
Herculis veram meruere laudem

Gesta per totum Latium probata
    plena triumphis,
Herculis nomen profitetur altum
Liberatorem fore putamus
Hunc ducem cunctis viciis acerbum
    juris amicum.

Secunda pars
Herculi debent superi favere
Quos pio semper veneratur ore
Herculi longam retinere vitam
    et Nestoris annos.
Herculi firmum stabilite regnum
Quod sibi magnis peperit periclis
Moribus sanctis [bene] cum vigore
    numina queso.
Herculem docti celebrent poete
Herculem dulces resonent camene
Concinant ympnos pueri puelle
    omnis et etas.
[Hercules] virtus tua publicetur
Jam potes magnos aperire sensus
Jam datur sacras reserare curas
    pectoris almi.
Hercules nobis tociens petite
Alter Alcides domitor ferarum
Victor humanus populo volente
    accipe sceptra.
Herculem justum facilem benignum
Predicat vates; super astra tollant*
Tot bonas artes variasque dotes
    principe dignas.
Ter quater nostri populi beati
Contingit talis quibus imperator
Nil potest quod [nos] vereamur esse
    Hercule salvo.
Auream certe patriam vocemus
Illa Saturni remeavit etas
Gaudium risus agitemus omnes
    Hercule rege. Amen.

            * * *

Prima pars
Ercole to be mentioned in all ages,
Ercole to be lauded all over the earth,
the well-born scion of the Este race,
    the noble hero,
at last, wishing to hold the reins of government,
received the reward of so great a labor.
Virtue, disturbed alas by what fates,
    rests happy.
Ercole's uprightness is worthy of honor,
Ercole's deeds have earned true praise,
approved of throughout all Italy
    full of triumphs,
he professes the exalted name of Hercules,
we think he will be a liberator,
this leader, harsh towards all vices,
    the friend of law.

Secunda pars
The gods ought to favor Ercole,
whom he always worships with pious mouth;
to keep long life for Ercole
    and Nestor's years.
Establish the secure reign for Ercole
that he has created for himself in great dangers
by most holy ways with vigor,
    ye gods, I beg you.
let learned poets celebrate Ercole,
let sweet Muses resound his name,
Let boys and girls sing hymns together
    and every age.
Ercole, let your virtue be bruited abroad;
now you may reveal your mighty thoughts,
now it is allowed to unlock the sacred cares
    of thy nurturing breast.
Ercole, whom we have so often prayed for,
another Alcides, tamer of wild beasts,
humane victor, by the people's will
    receive the scepter.
Ercole the just, easygoing and kind,
the seer proclaims; let them exalt above the stars
so many liberal arts and various gifts
    worthy of a prince.
Thrice and four times are our peoples blessed
to whom such a commander befalls.
Nothing for us to fear can happen
    while Ercole is safe.
Let us for sure call our country golden:
that age of Saturn has returned;
let us all stir up joy and laughter under
    King Ercole. Amen.

Comments. *Something wrong in this line; what is the subject of *tollant*? At a pinch one might say *astra*, "let the stars exalt up above," *super* being adverbial, but the expression would be very strange.

Notes. M. 1, B, labeled "Bassus contratenor." Mm. 23–25, A, "stirps." M. 25, S, "stirps." M. 30, A, "imperij." Mm. 30–32, A, "imperij." Mm. 30–35, T, "imperij." Mm. 30–31, B, "imperij." Mm. 145–47, A, "tenere." Mm. 191–92, A, "dulcedo." Mm. 201–6, T, "magnos potes." Mm. 281–85, T, "veremur." Mm. 265–68, B, "saturus." Mm. 269–74, B, "remeat."

31. Salve Regina

Primary source. MunBS 3154, fols. 89r–93r, Jo.

Concordant source. DresSL 1/D/505, pp. 431–35 (incomplete, lacks the following sections: "Salve

Regina," "Ad te clamamus," "Ad te suspiramus," "Eya ergo," and "O dulcis Virgo"; also lacks the S and B of the "advocata nostra" and "Et Jesum" sections).

Modern editions. Gerber, 4–13. Noblitt, 81:11–24.

Text source, main text. AH, 50:318–19.

Main text

Salve Regina [mater] misericordie:
Vita, dulcedo, et spes nostra, salve.
Ad te clamamus, exules, filii Eve.
Ad te suspiramus, gementes et flentes
In hac lacrimarum valle.
Eya ergo, advocata nostra,
Illos tuos misericordes oculos ad nos converte.
Et Jesum, benedictum fructum ventris tui,
Nobis post hoc exilium ostende.
O clemens, O pia,
O dulcis Virgo Maria.

* * *

Hail Queen of Mercy,
our life, sweetness, and hope, hail.
To you we cry, exiles, children of Eve.
To you we sigh, lamenting and weeping
in this vale of tears.
Therefore, our advocate,
turn your merciful eyes on us.
And after this exile, reveal Jesus to us,
the blessed fruit of thy womb.
O merciful, O holy,
O sweet virgin Mary.

Text source, cantus firmus text. Lines 1–3, benediction for peace, LU 1867. Lines 4–7, verse 6 of the hymn for Passion Sunday, "Vexilla regis." Lines 8–9, antiphon for the common of Apostles and Evangelists out of Paschal Time, LU 1111. Lines 10–12, hymn to Christ the King, LU 586. Lines 13–14, verse 9 of the sequence "Veni Sancte Spiritus," LU 880–81.

Cantus firmus text

Da pacem, Domine, in diebus nostris;
Quia non est alius, qui pugnet pro nobis,
Nisi tu, Deus, noster.
O crux, ave, spes unica,
Hoc passionis tempore.
Auge piis justitiam
Reisque dona veniam.
Vos amici mei estis si feceritis,
Que precipio vobis, dicit Dominus.
Gloria, laus et honor tibi sit,
Rex Christe redemptor:
Cui puerile decus prompsit Osanna pium.
Da tuis fidelibus in te confidentibus
Sacrum septenarium.

* * *

Give us peace, O Lord, in our time;
for there is no one else who would fight for us,
except you, Lord.
Hail, O cross, our only hope,
in this time of the Passion.
Extend justice to the holy
and grant pardon to the guilty.
You will be my friends if you do
what I command you, says the Lord.
Glory, praise and honor be yours,
O Christ, King and redeemer:
for whom the faithful, like children, utter Osanna.
Give your faithful, trusting in you,
the seven sacraments.

Note. M. 6, A, note 3, minim; should be a semiminim.

Variants in DresSL 1/D/505. M. 139, A, note 2 to m. 140, note 1, breve, semibreve. M. 141, T, note 1 to m. 142, note 1, ligature. M. 142, T, note 1 to m. 143, note 1, no ligature. M. 143, A, notes 1–2, no ligature. M. 145, A, notes 3–4, minim, minim. M. 156, T, note 5 to m. 157, note 2, no ligature. M. 158, A, notes 1–2, ligature. M. 159, A, notes 1–2, no ligature. M. 164, T, notes 1–2, no ligature. M. 167, A, note 2 to m. 168, note 1, ligature. M. 170, T, note 2 to m. 171, note 2, dotted breve. M. 179, T, notes 1–2, no ligature. M. 182, T, note 3, a. M. 184, T, note 4, e'. M. 188, A, notes 1–2, dotted semibreve. M. 190, A, note 5 to m. 191, note 3, semibreve, semiminim, semiminim.

M. 209, A, note 4, no ♭. M. 213, A, note 1 to m. 215, note 1, ligature. M. 215, S, note 1 to m. 216, note 1, ligature. M. 216, B, note 1 to m. 218, note 1, ligature. M. 218, T, note 1 to m. 219, note 1, ligature. M. 219, B, note 1, semibreve d, semibreve d. M. 221, T, note 1 to m. 222, note 1, ligature. M. 222, S, notes 4–5, semibreve e'. M. 223, S, note 1 to m. 224, note 4, dotted colored semibreve f', semiminim d', dotted colored semibreve e', semiminim f', dotted colored semibreve g', semiminim a'. M. 223, A, note 1 to m. 225, note 1, ligature. M. 227, S, note 3, semibreve e'. M. 230, A, note 4 to m. 231, note 2, minor color. M. 231, T, note 3 to m. 232, note 3, breve c'. M. 235, S, note 1 to m. 236, note 1, ligature. M. 237, A, note 2, no ♭. M. 239, S, notes 2–3, minor color. M. 239, A, notes 2–3, minor color. M. 241, A, note 1, no ♭. M. 242, T, note 1 to m. 244, note 1, ligature. M. 244, S, note 1 to m. 246, note 1, ligature. M. 244, T, note 1, no ♭. M. 246, S, note 1, ♭. M. 251, T, note 1 to m. 252, note 1, ligature. M. 251, S, notes 1–2, missing; this is a haplographic mistake. M. 254, B, note 1 to m. 256, note 1, ligature. M. 257, B, note 1, no ligature. M. 259, A, notes 2–3, minor color. M. 261, A, note 2, no ♭. M. 262, S, note 1 to m. 263, note 2, minor color. M. 264,

T, note 1 to m. 265, note 1, ligature.   M. 265, S, notes 5–6, semibreve e'.   M. 265, A, note 3 to m. 266, note 3, breve b.   M. 266, T, note 1, no ligature.   M. 269, S, note 2, minim b'.   M. 270, T, note 1 to m. 271, note 1, ligature.   M. 270, B, note 1, B.   M. 274, A, note 1, no ♭.   M. 276, S, note 3, semiminim b', semiminim a'.   M. 277, S, notes 1–2, no ligature.   M. 277, A, note 2, no ♭.   M. 282, T, note 2, no ♭.   M. 283, B, note 1 to m. 286, note 1, double long.   M. 286, A, note 1, long d'.   M. 287, B, key signature is E♭ for the "O Clemens" section.   M. 293, B, note 1, minim A.   M. 293, B, notes 2–3, minor color.   M. 296, B, note 4 to m. 297, note 2, minor color.   M. 296, B, notes 2–3, minor color.   M. 298, T, note 1 to m. 299, note 1, dotted long; this is a mistake.

M. 300, A, note 4 to m. 301, note 2, minor color.   M. 303, A, notes 3–4, minim c', semiminim b, semiminim c'.   M. 304, A, note 3 to m. 305, note 2, minor color.   M. 305, S, notes 4–5, semibreve e'.   M. 305, A, note 3, missing.   M. 306, T, note 1 to m. 307, note 1, no ligature.   M. 306, T, note 1, semibreve g', minim g'.   M. 307, S, notes 3–4, minor color.   M. 307, T, notes 4–5, semibreve c'.

Notes

1. For further reading on *musica ficta,* see: Karol Berger, *Musica Ficta* (Cambridge; New York: Cambridge University Press, 1987); Nicholas Routley, "A Practical Guide to Musica Ficta," *Early Music* 13 (1985): 59–71; Margaret Bent, "Diatonic Ficta," *Early Music History* 4 (1984): 1–48; Bent, "Musica Recta and Musica Ficta," *Musica Disciplina* 26 (1972): 73–100; Thomas Noblitt, "Chromatic Cross-Relations and Editorial Musica Ficta in Masses of Obrecht," *Tijdschrift van de Vereiniging voor Nederlandse Muziek-geschiedenis* 32 (1982): 30–44; and Peter Whitney Urquhart, "Three Sample Problems of Editorial Accidentals in Chansons by Busnoys and Ockeghem," in *Music in Renaissance Cities and Courts: Studies in Honor of Lewis Lockwood,* ed. Anthony M. Cummings and Jesse Ann Owens (Warren, Mich.: Harmonie Park Press, 1997), 465–81.

2. For those interested in pursuing the issue of text underlay, numerous excellent studies exist; see: Allan Atlas, "Paolo Luchini's *Della Musica:* A Little-Known Source for Text Underlay from the Late Sixteenth Century," *Journal of Musicology* 2 (1983): 62–80; Margaret Bent, "Text Setting in Sacred Music of the Early 15th Century: Evidence and Implications," in *Musik und Text in der Mehrstimmigkeit des 14. und 15. Jahrhunderts,* ed. Ursula Günther and Ludwig Finscher (Basel: Bärenreiter, 1984), 291–326; Howard M. Brown, " 'Lord, have mercy upon us': Early Sixteenth-Century Scribal Practice and the Polyphonic Kyrie," *Transactions of the Society for Textual Scholarship* 2 (1985): 93–110; Brown, "In Alamire's Workshop. Notes on Scribal Practice in the Early Sixteenth Century," in *Datierung und Filiation von Musikhandschriften der Josquin-Zeit,* ed. Ludwig Finscher, Wolfenbüttler Forschungen, vol. 26 (Wiesbaden: Harrassowitz, 1983), 15–64; Brown, "Text Underlay," in *A Chansonnier from the Time of Lorenzo the Magnificent* (Chicago: University of Chicago Press, 1983), 168–80; Gareth R. K. Curtis, "Brussels, Bibliothèque Royale MS. 5557 and the Texting of Dufay's *Ecce ancilla Domini* and *Ave regina caelorum* Masses," *Acta Musicologica* 51 (1979): 73–86; Rebecca L. Gerber, "Ligature and Notational Practices as Determining Factors in the Text Underlay of Fifteenth-Century Sacred Music," *Studi Musicali* 20 (1991): 45–67; Peter Gülke, "Et incarnatus est - Zur Entwicklung des Wort-Ton-Verhältnisses in der Meßkomposition des 15. Jahrhunderts anhand einer zentralen Passage (glichzeitig öffentlicher Vortrag in der Augusteerhalle der Bibliotheca Augusta)," in *Musik und Text in der Mehrstimmigkeit des 14. und 15. Jahrhunderts,* ed. Ursula Günter and Ludwig Finscher (Kassel: Bärenreiter, 1984), 351–82; Don Harrán, "In Pursuit of Origins: The Earliest Writing on Text Underlay (c. 1440)," *Acta Musicologica* 50 (1978): 217–40; Harrán, "New Light on the Question of Text Underlay Prior to Zarlino," *Acta Musicologica* 45 (1973): 24–56; Harrán, *Word-Tone Relations in Musical Thought from Antiquity to the Seventeenth Century* (Neuhausen-Stuttgart: American Institute of Musicology, 1986); Mary S. Lewis, "Zarlino's Theories of Text Underlay as Illustrated in his Motet Book of 1549," *Notes* 42 (1985): 239–67; Chris Mass, "Text Underlay," *Tijdschrift van de Vereniging voor Nederlandse Muziek-geschiedenis* 24 (1974): 69–79; Leeman L. Perkins, "Toward a Rational Approach to Text Placement in the Secular Music of Dufay's Time," in *Papers Read at the Dufay Quincentenary Conference, Brooklyn College, December 6–7, 1974,* ed. Allan W. Atlas (Brooklyn, N.Y.: Brooklyn College, 1976), 102–14 and 152–63; Alejandro E. Planchart, "Parts with Words and Without Words: The Evidence for Multiple Texts in Fifteenth-Century Masses," in *Studies in the Performance of Late Mediaeval Music,* ed. Stanley Boorman (Cambridge: Cambridge University Press, 1983), 227–51; and Gaspar Stoquerus, *De musica verbali libri duo,* ed. Albert C. Rotola, S.J. (Lincoln, Neb. and London: University of Nebraska Press, 1988).

Plate 1. "Festum nunc celebre" (no. 7), MunBS 3154, fol. 150v. (Courtesy of Munich, Bayerische Staatsbibliothek.)

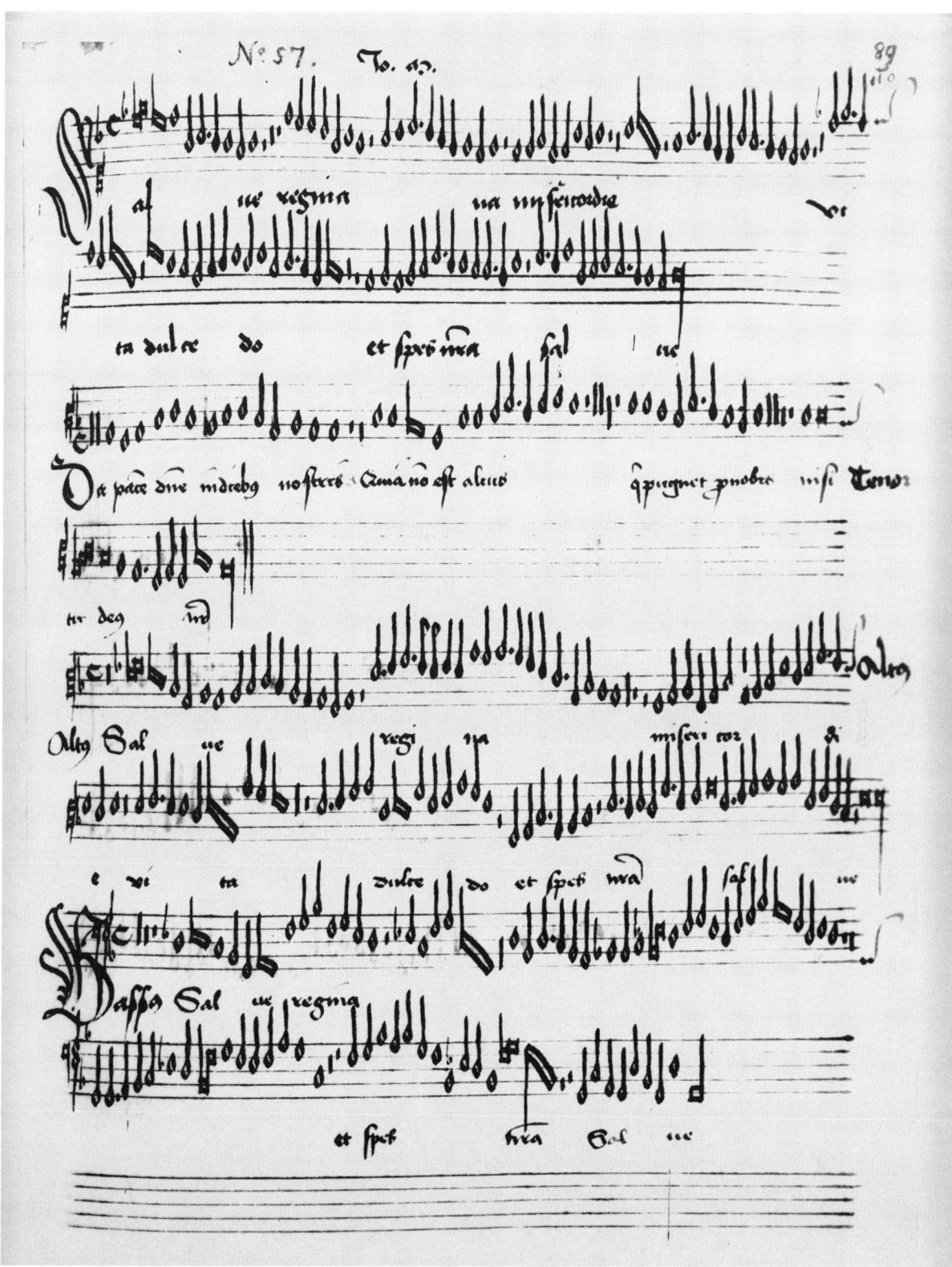

Plate 2. "Salve Regina" (no. 31), MunBS 3154, fol. 89r. (Courtesy of Munich, Bayerische Staatsbibliothek.)

Hymns, Magnificats, Motets, and Passions

1. Audi, benigne conditor

Johannes Martini

2. Aures ad nostras

Johannes Brebis
and Johannes Martini

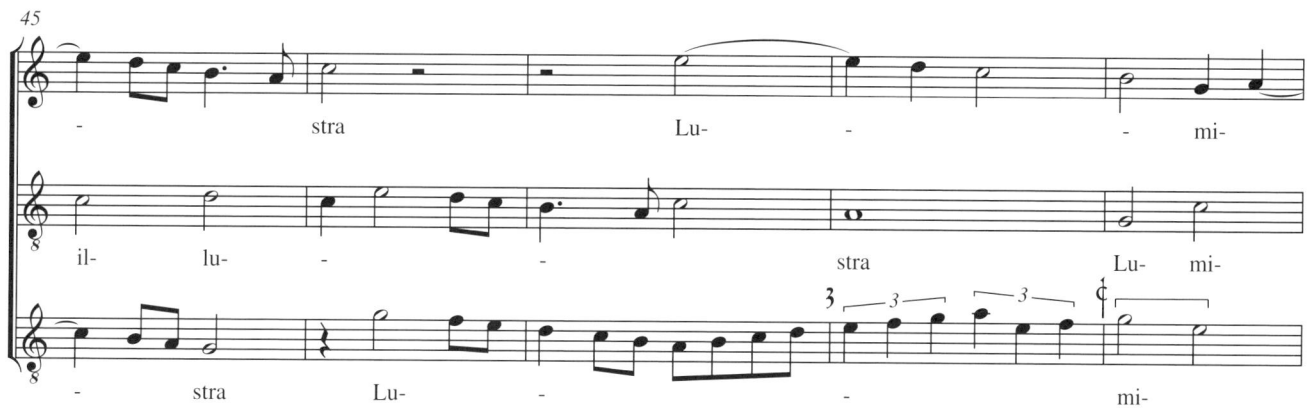

3. Ave maris stella

Johannes Martini

4. Deus tuorum militum (1)

Johannes Brebis
and Johannes Martini

5. Deus tuorum militum (2)

Johannes Martini

6. Exultet celum laudibus

Johannes Martini

7. Festum nunc celebre

Johannes Martini

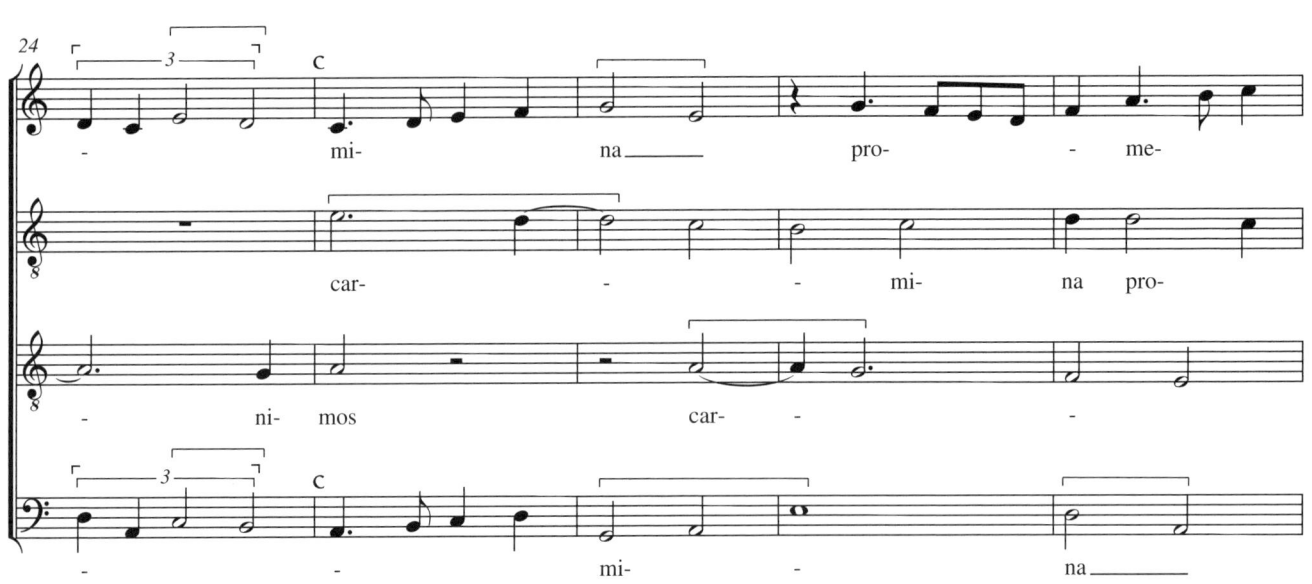

8. Iste confessor

Johannes Martini

9. Jesu, corona virginum

Johannes Martini

10. Sanctorum meritis

Johannes Brebis
and Johannes Martini

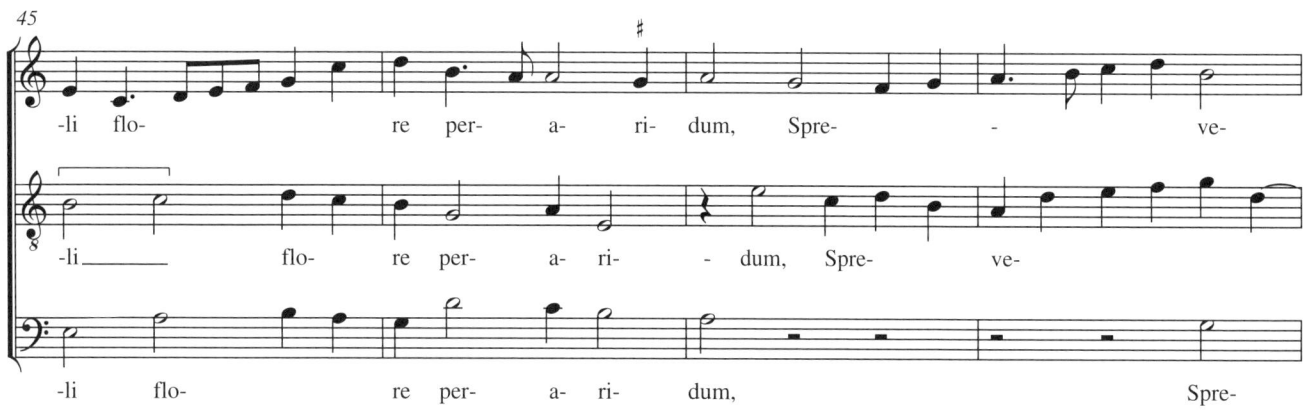
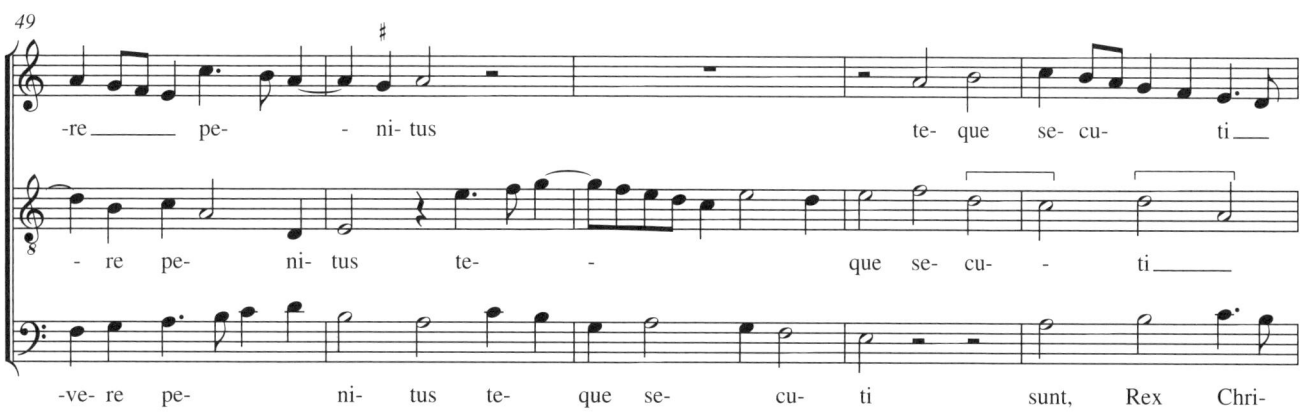

11. Tibi, Christe, splendor

Johannes Martini

12. Vexilla regis

Johannes Brebis
and Johannes Martini

32

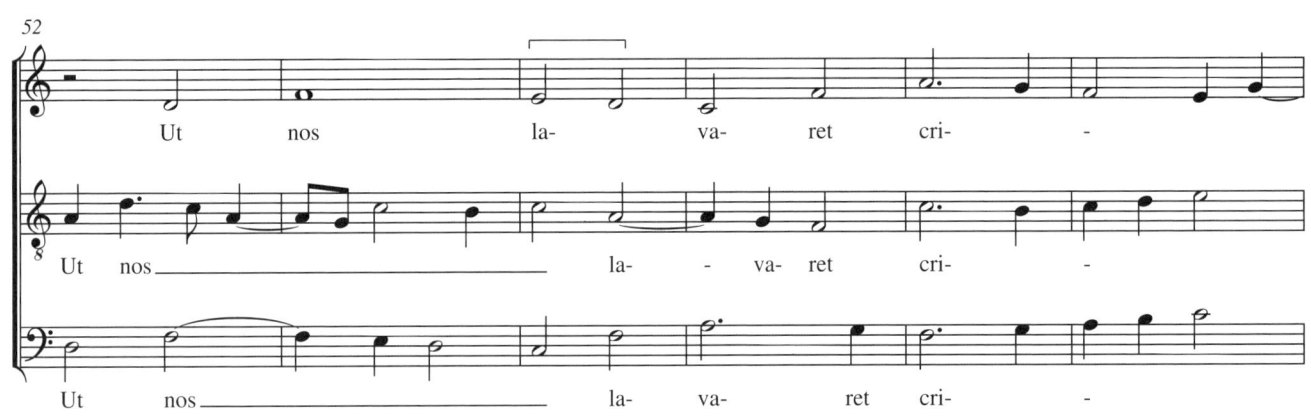

13. Magnificat 1. toni

Johannes Martini

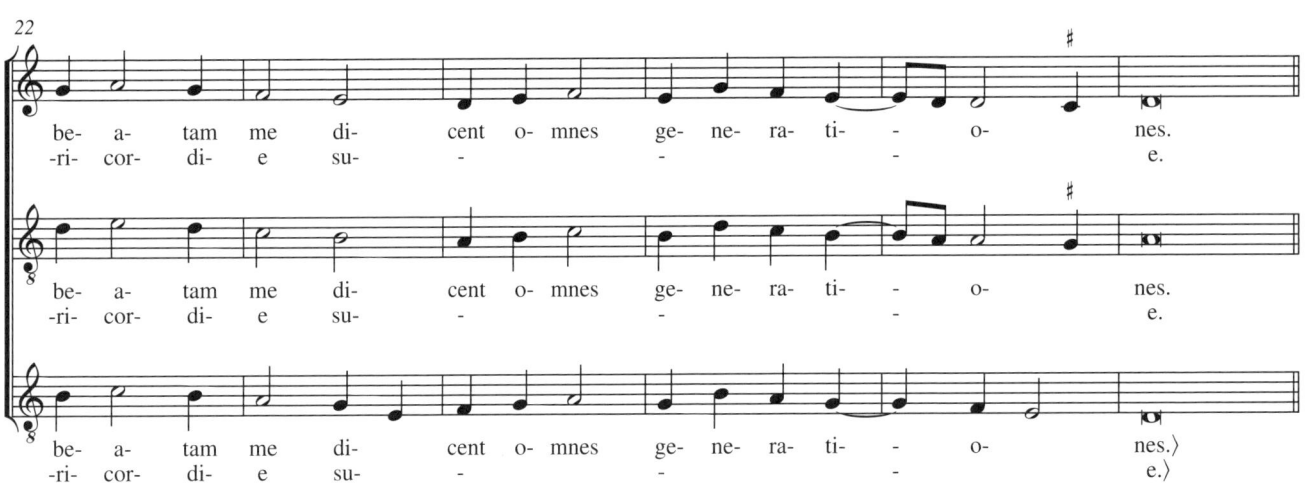
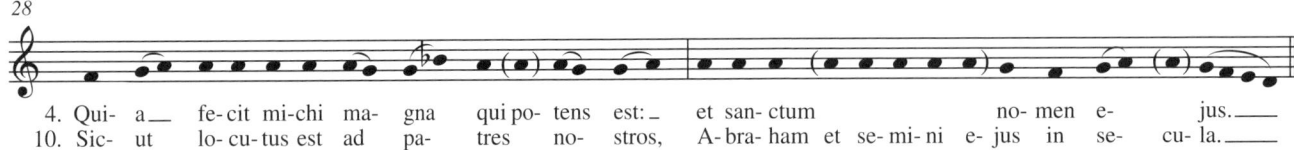

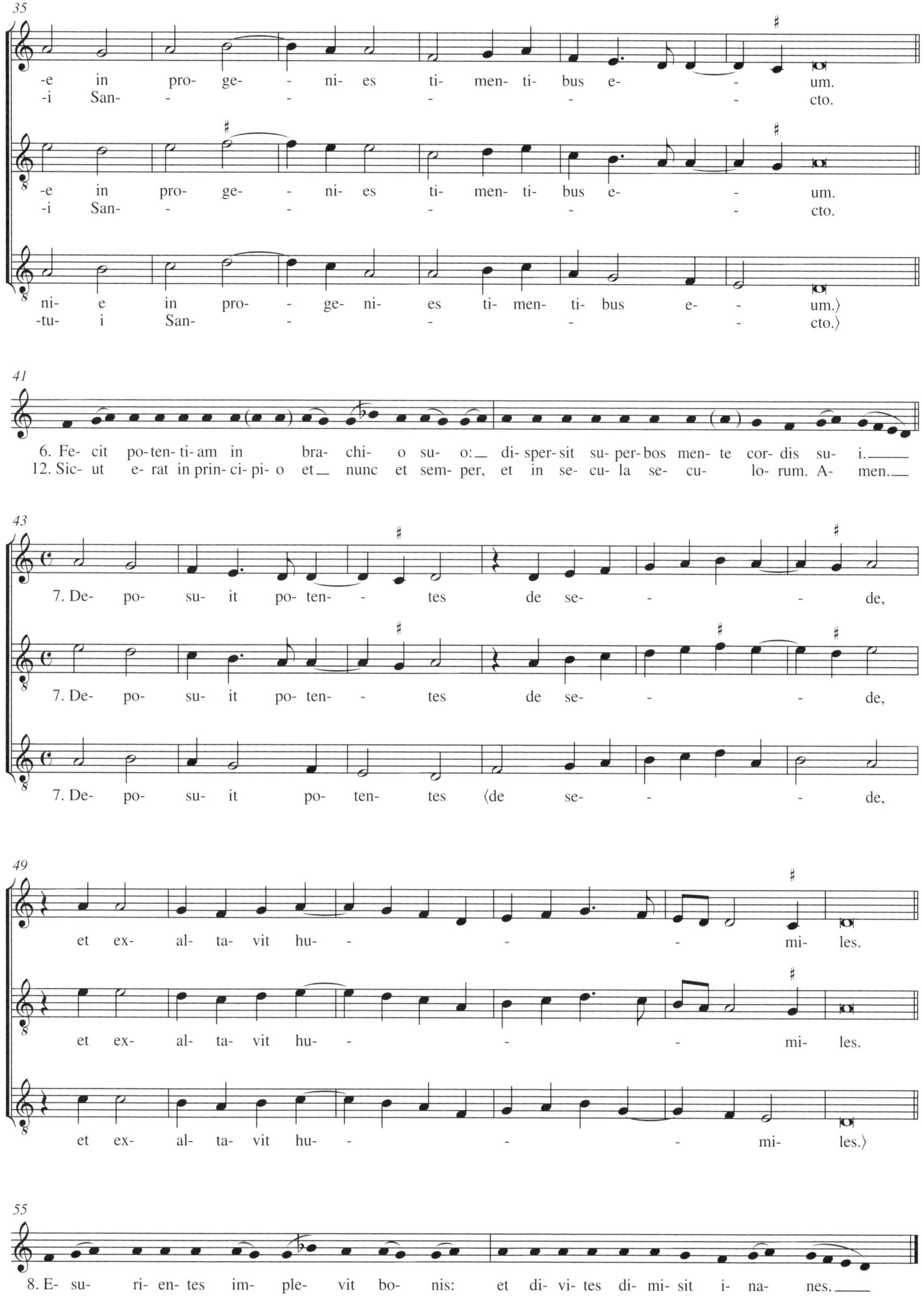
35
-e in pro- ge- - ni- es ti- men- ti- bus e- - um.
-i San- - - - - - cto.
-e in pro- ge- - ni- es ti- men- ti- bus e- - um.
-i San- - - - - - cto.
ni- e in pro- - ge- ni- es ti- men- ti- bus e- - um.〉
-tu- i San- - - - - cto.〉
41
6. Fe- cit po- ten- ti- am in bra- chi- o su- o: di- sper- sit su- per- bos men- te cor- dis su- i.
12. Sic- ut e- rat in prin- ci- pi- o et nunc et sem- per, et in se- cu- la se- cu- lo- rum. A- men.
43
7. De- po- su- it po- ten- - tes de se- - - de,
7. De- po- su- it po- ten- - tes de se- - - de,
7. De- po- su- it po- ten- tes 〈de se- - - de,
49
et ex- al- ta- vit hu- - - - mi- les.
et ex- al- ta- vit hu- - - - mi- les.
et ex- al- ta- vit hu- - - - mi- les.〉
55
8. E- su- ri- en- tes im- ple- vit bo- nis: et di- vi- tes di- mi- sit i- na- nes.

14. Magnificat 3. toni (1)

Johannes Martini

15. Magnificat 3. toni (2)

Johannes Martini

46

48

197
i San-
tu- i⟩ San-
203
cto.
cto.
cto.
cto, ⟨-cto.⟩
210
Sic- ut e- rat in prin- ci- pi- o, et nunc, et sem- per, et in se- cu- la se- cu- lo- rum. A- men.

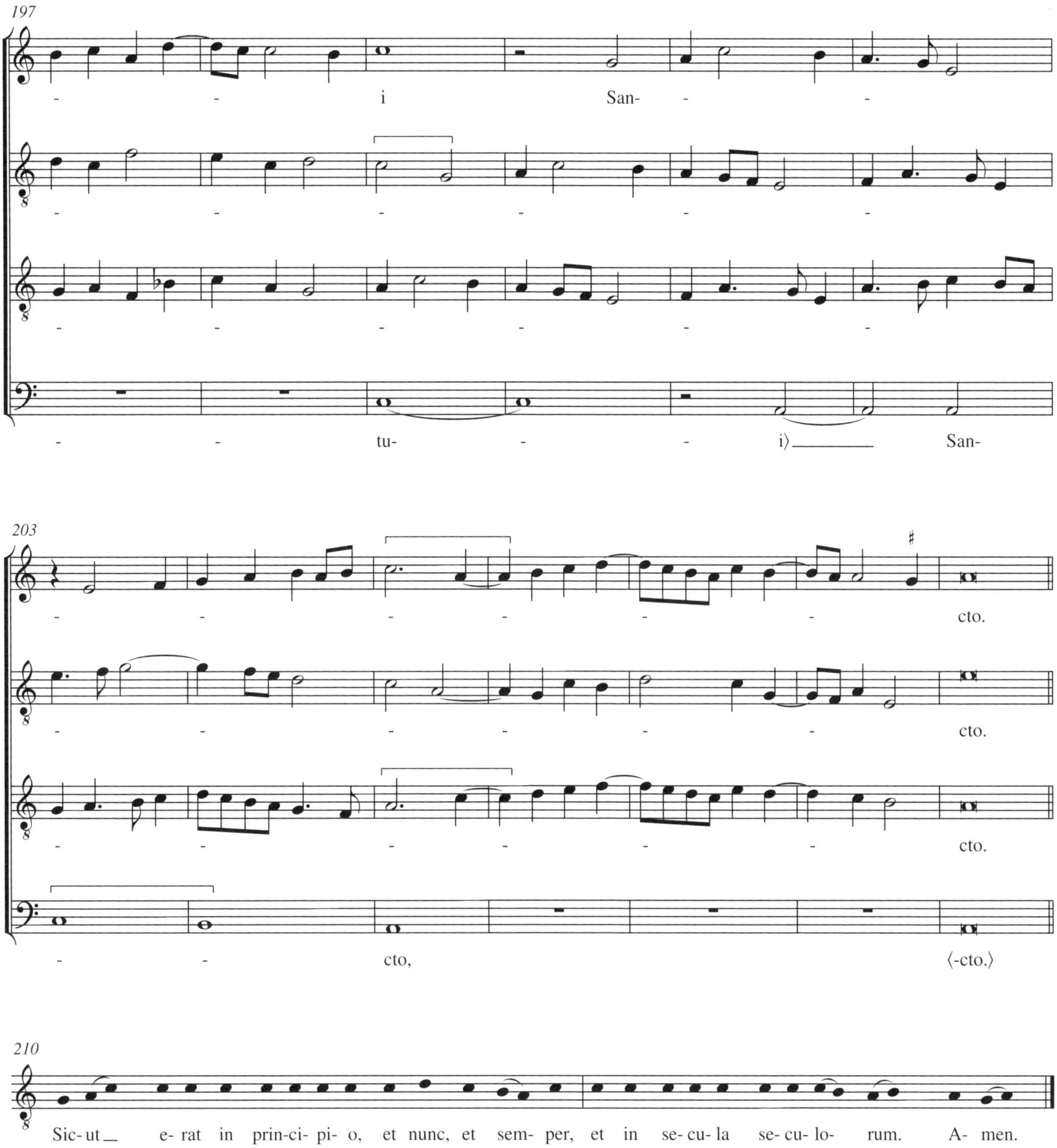

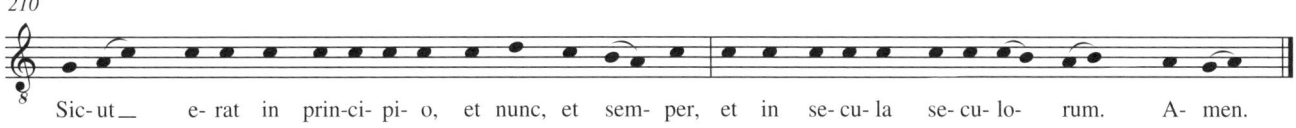

16. Magnificat 4. toni

Johannes Martini

©2009 by the Biblioteca Apostolica Vaticana. All rights reserved.
Used with permission.

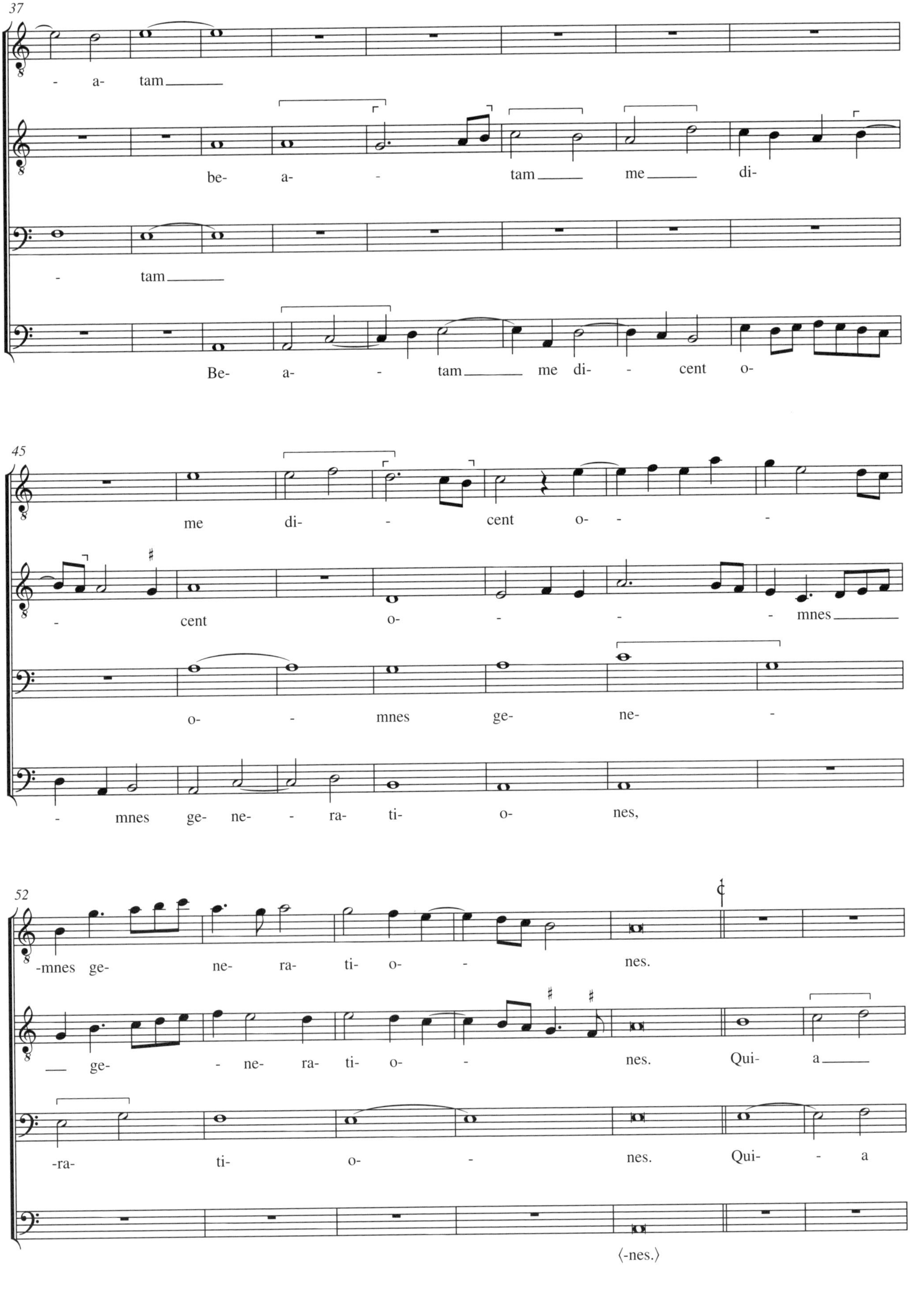
37
- a- tam
be- a- - tam me di-
- tam
Be- a- - tam me di- - cent o-
45
me di- - cent o- - -
- cent o- - - - mnes
o- - mnes ge- ne- -
- mnes ge- ne- - ra- ti- o- nes,
52
-mnes ge- ne- ra- ti- o- - nes.
ge- - ne- ra- ti- o- - nes. Qui- a
-ra- ti- o- - nes. Qui- - a
⟨-nes.⟩

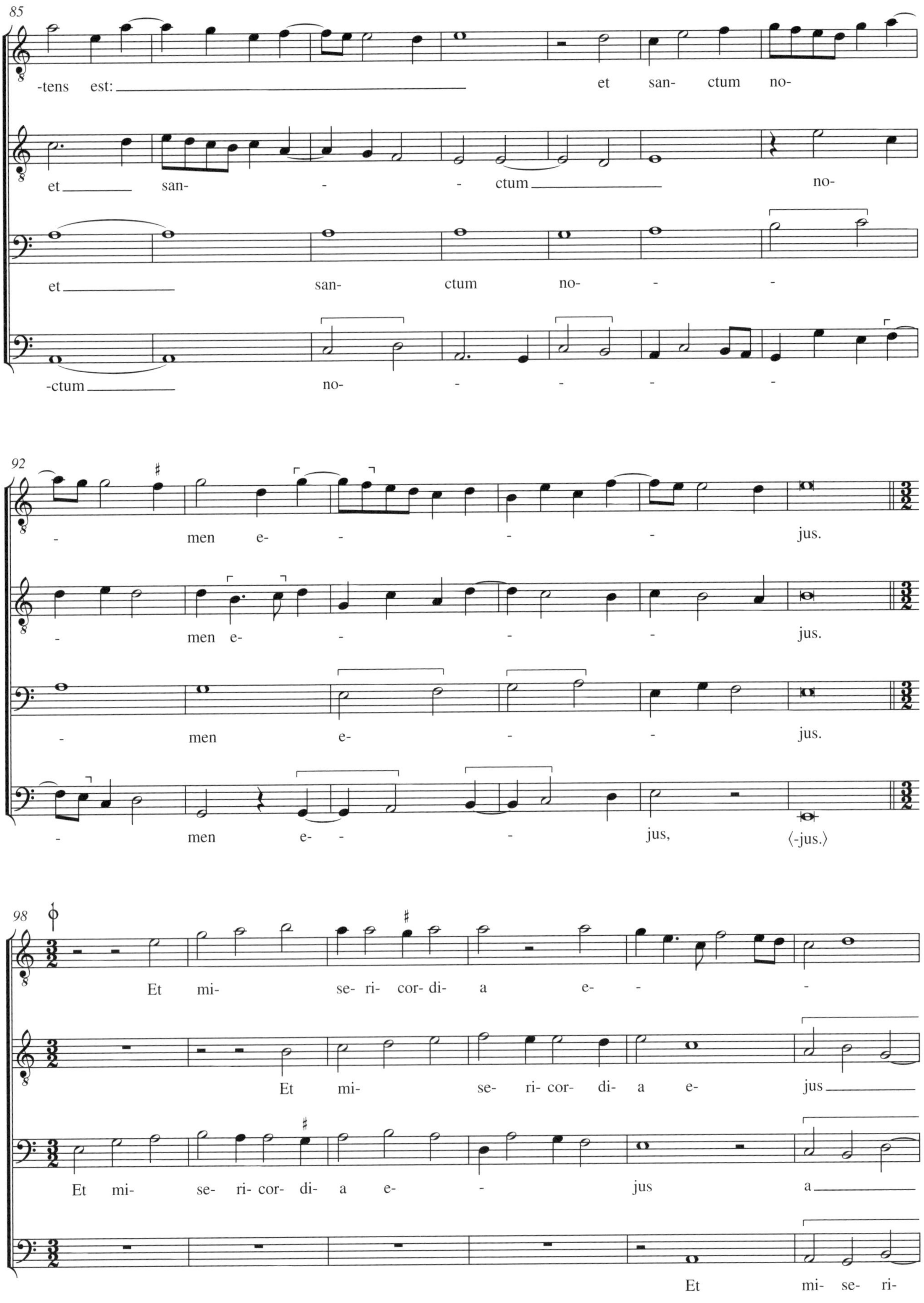
85
-tens est: et san- ctum no-
et san- - - ctum no-
et san- ctum no- - -
-ctum no- - - - -
92
- men e- - - - jus.
- men e- - - - jus.
- men e- - - jus.
- men e- - jus, ⟨-jus.⟩
98
Et mi- se- ri- cor- di- a e- - -
Et mi- se- ri- cor- di- a e- jus
Et mi- se- ri- cor- di- a e- - jus a
Et mi- se- ri-

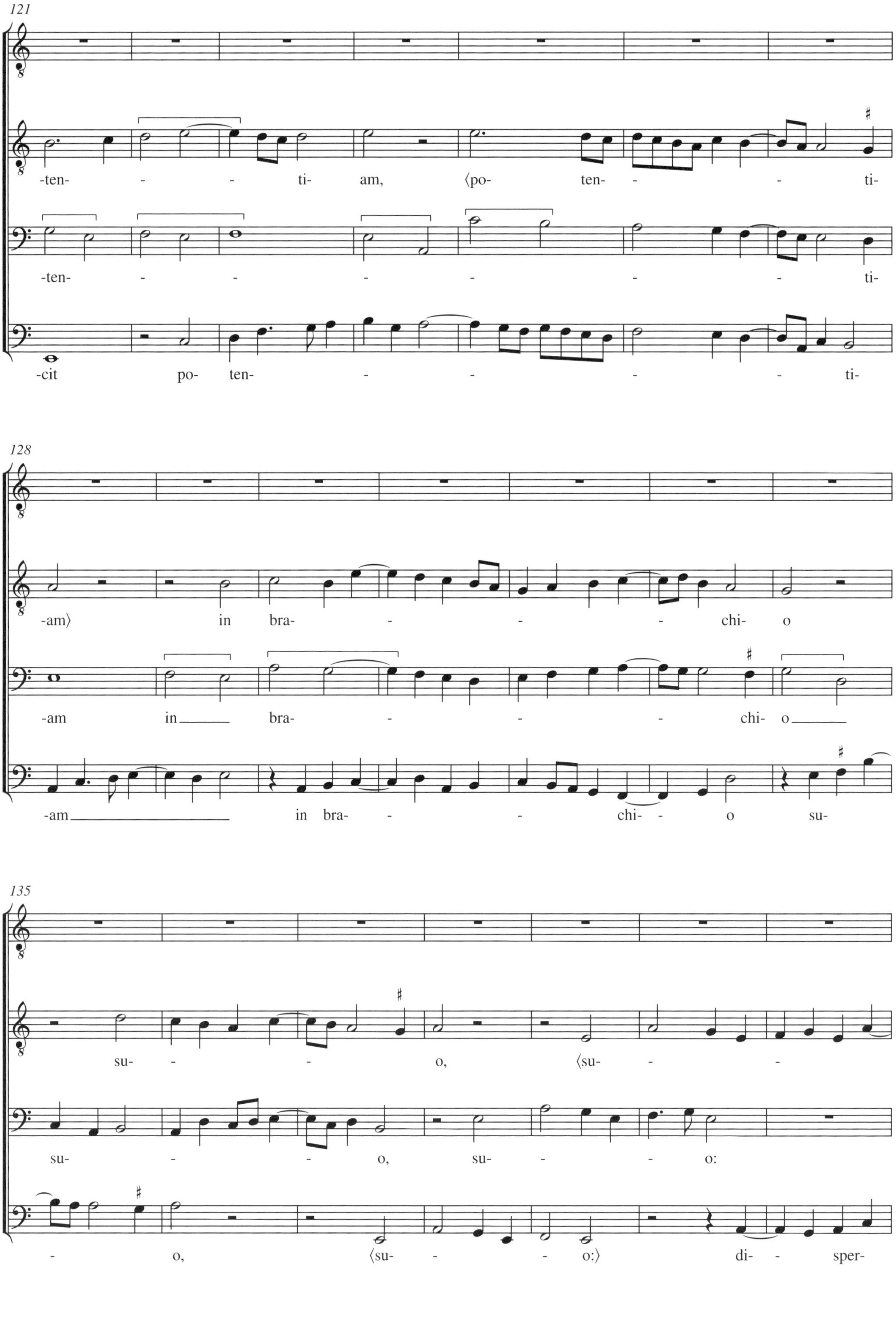
121
-ten- - - ti- am, ⟨po- ten- - - ti-
-ten- - - - - - - ti-
-cit po- ten- - - - - ti-
128
-am⟩ in bra- - - - chi- o
-am in bra- - - - chi- o
-am in bra- - chi- - o su-
135
su- - - o, ⟨su- - -
su- - - o, su- - - o:
- o, ⟨su- - - o:⟩ di- - sper-

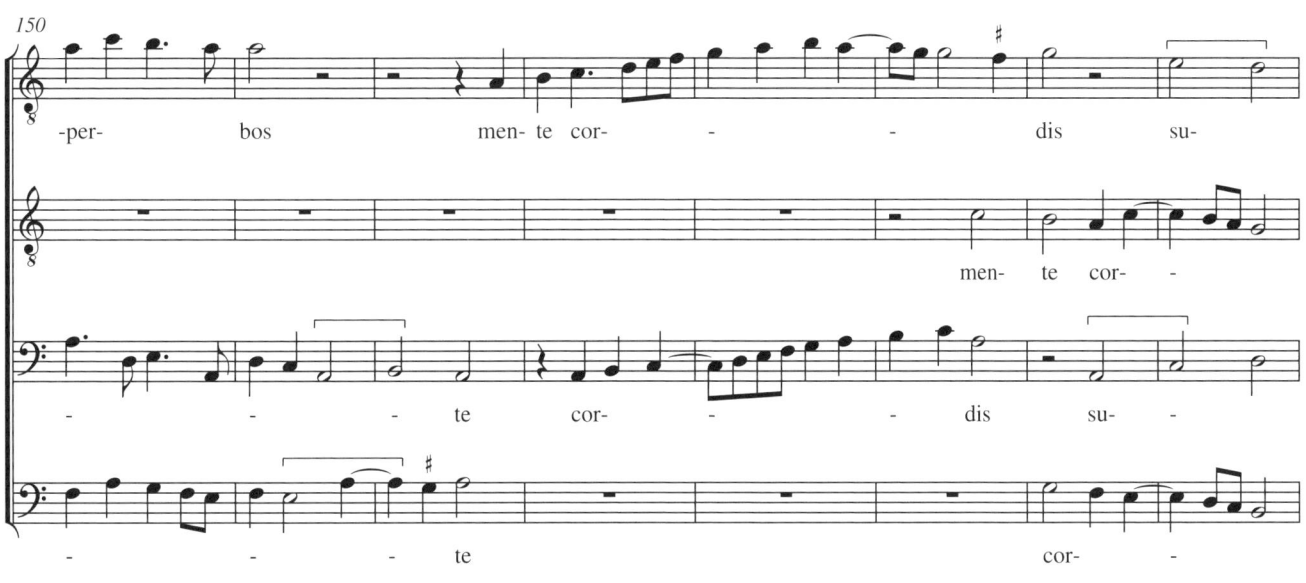

62

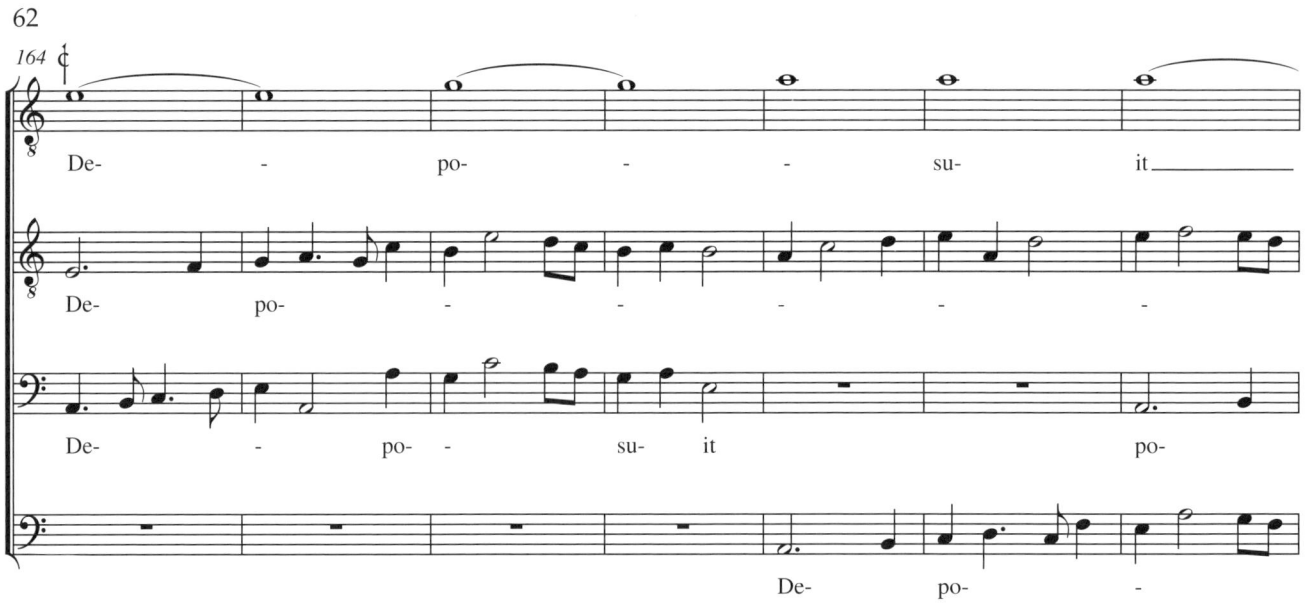

64

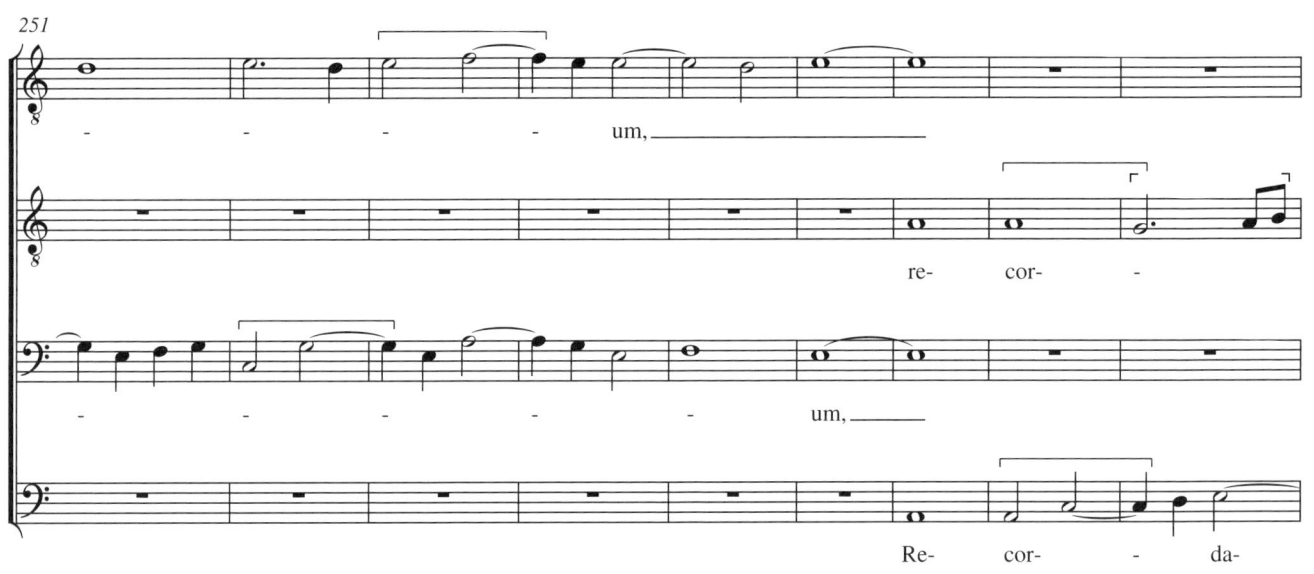

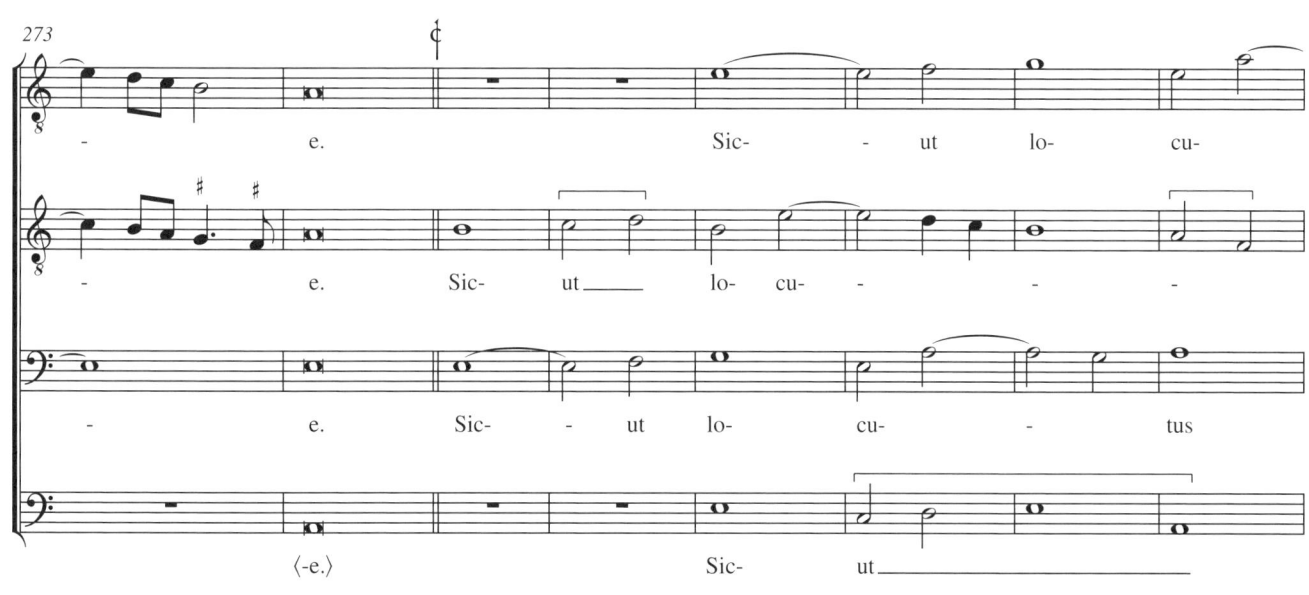
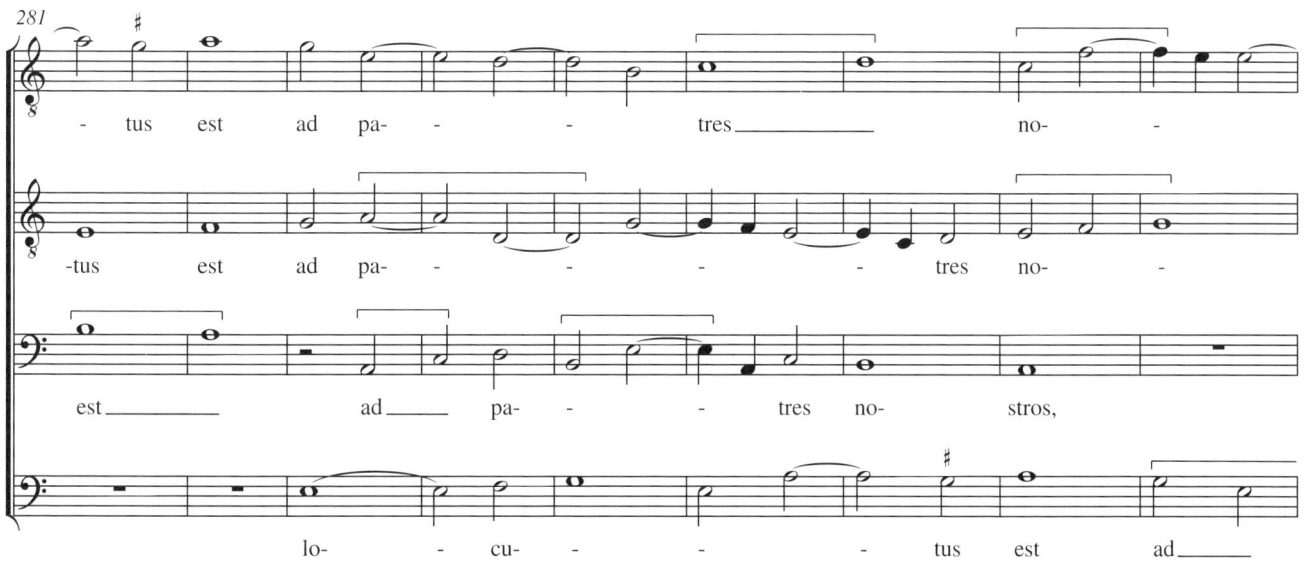

17. Magnificat 6. toni

Johannes Martini

©2009 by the Biblioteca Apostolica Vaticana. All rights reserved.
Used with permission.

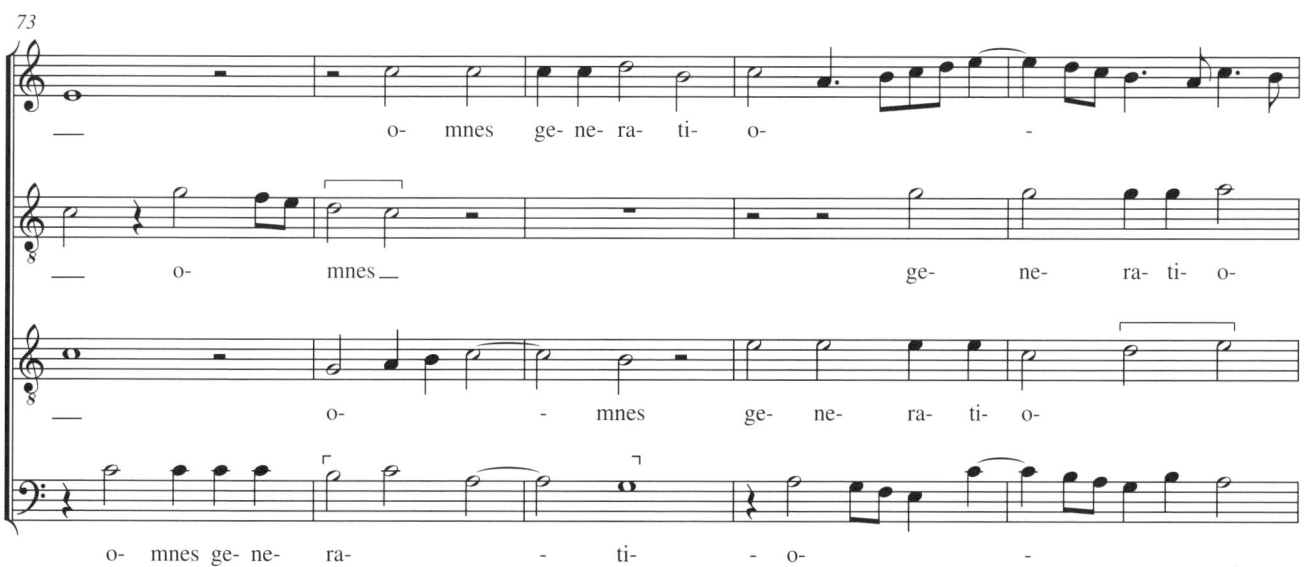
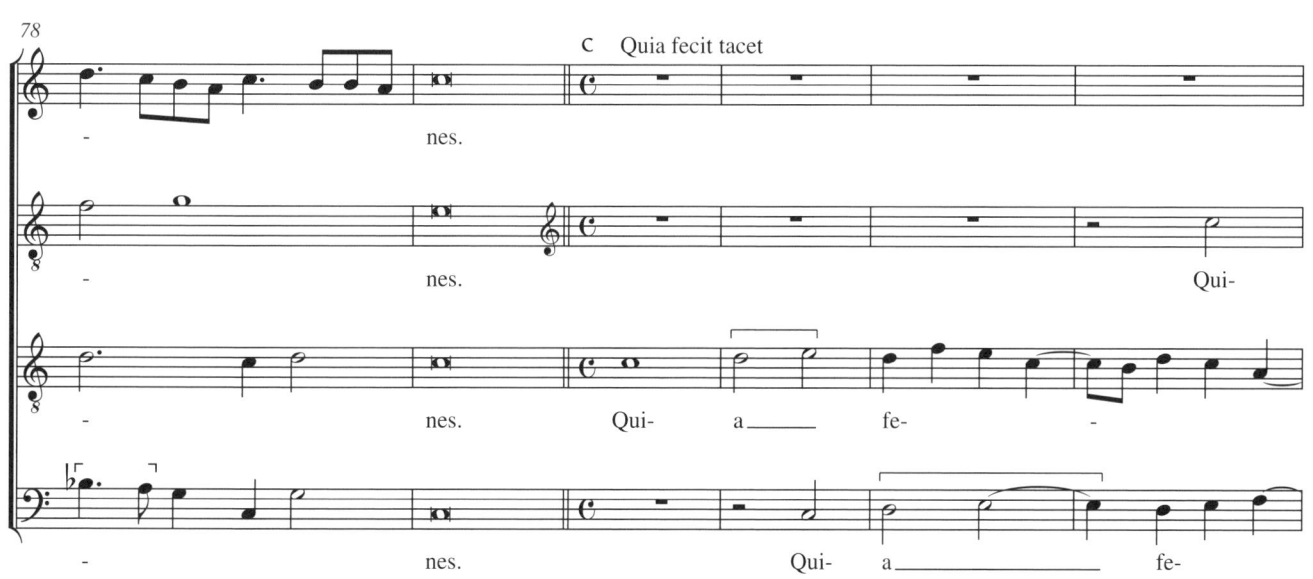

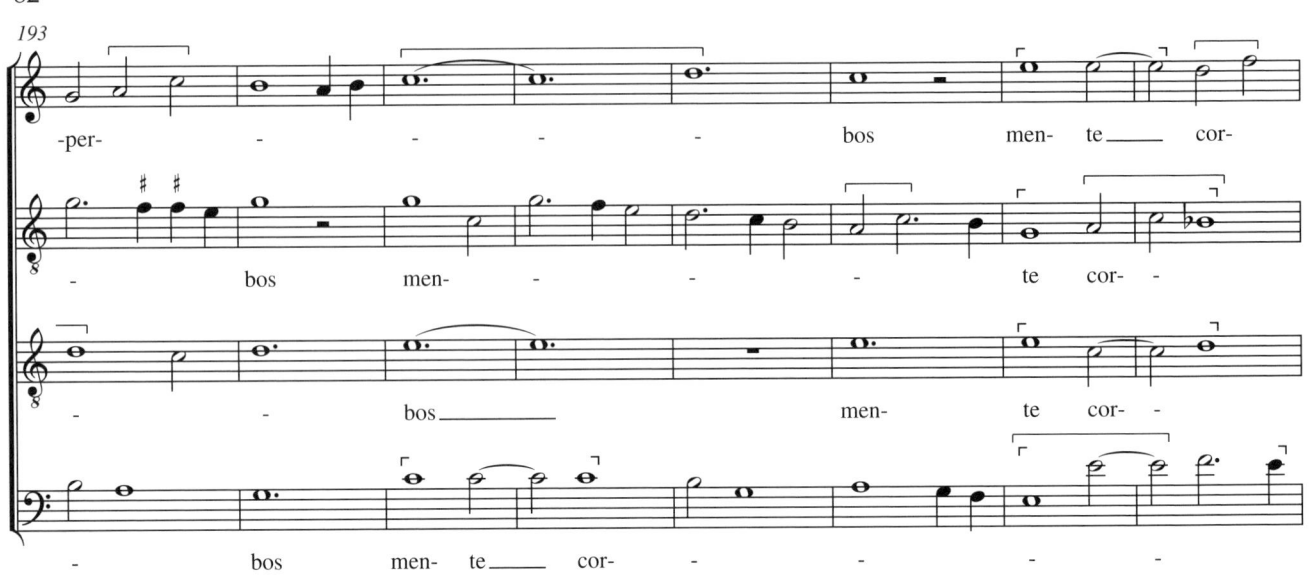

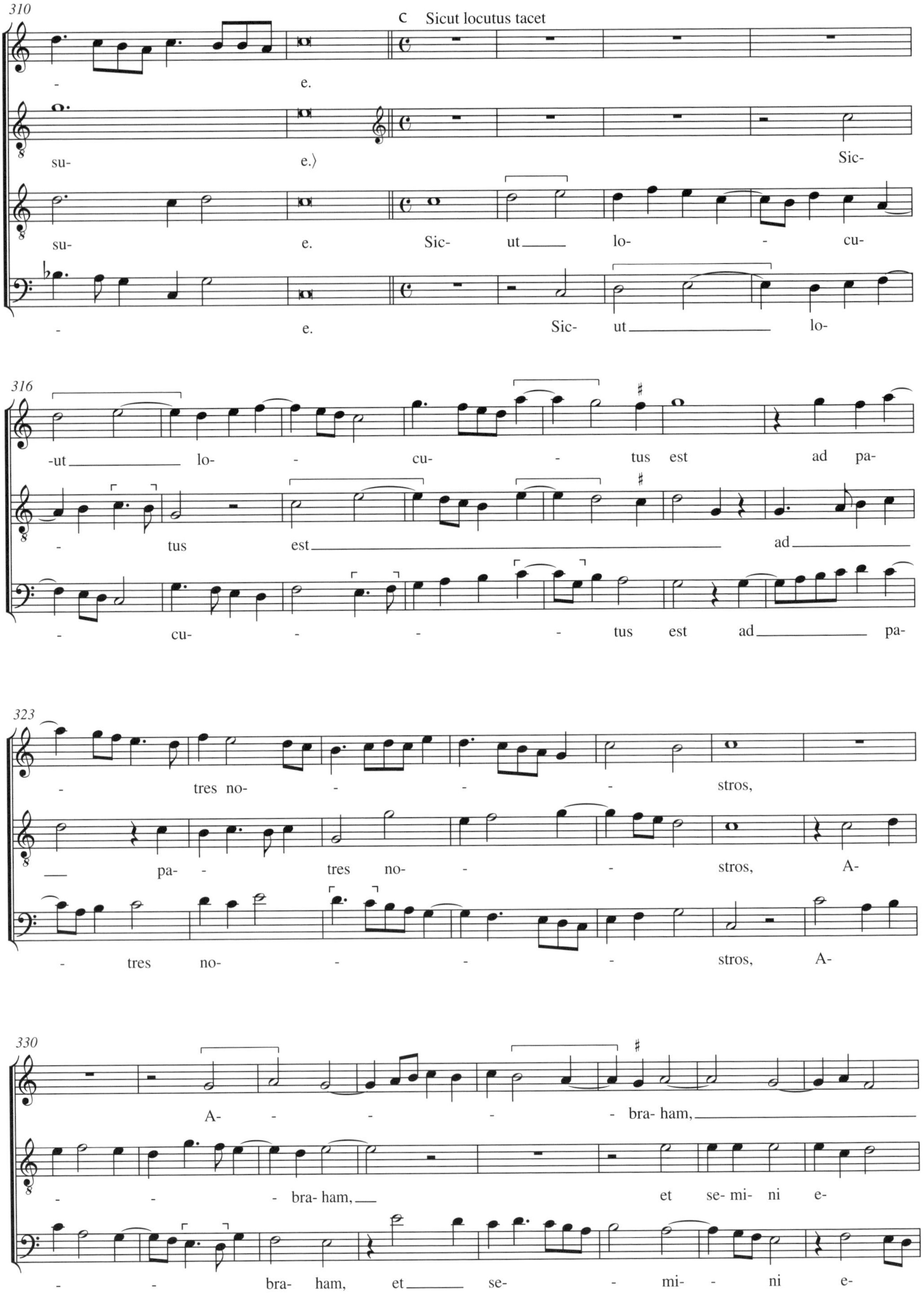
310
C Sicut locutus tacet
- e.
su- e.〉 Sic-
su- e. Sic- ut lo- - cu-
- e. Sic- ut lo-
316
CT
T
B
-ut lo- - cu- - tus est ad pa-
- tus est ad
- cu- - - - tus est ad pa-
323
- tres no- - - - stros,
pa- - tres no- - - stros, A-
- tres no- - - - stros, A-
330
A- - - - bra- ham,
- - - bra- ham, et se- mi- ni e-
- - bra- ham, et se- - mi- - ni e-

18. Magnificat 6. toni

Johannes Brebis

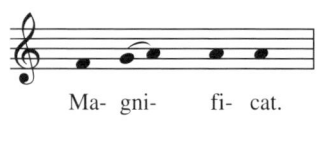
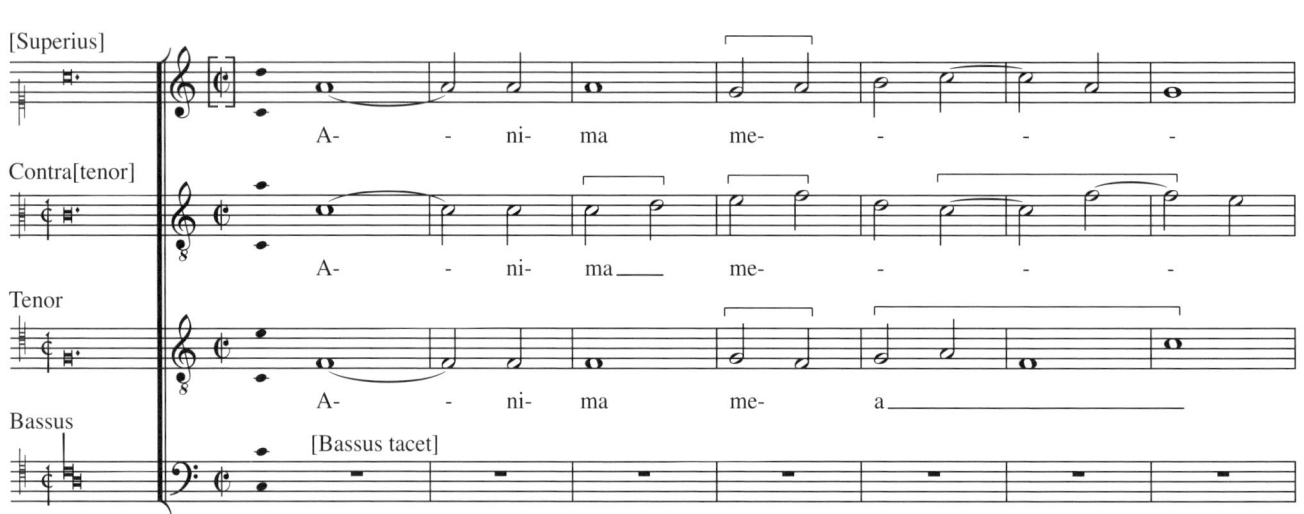

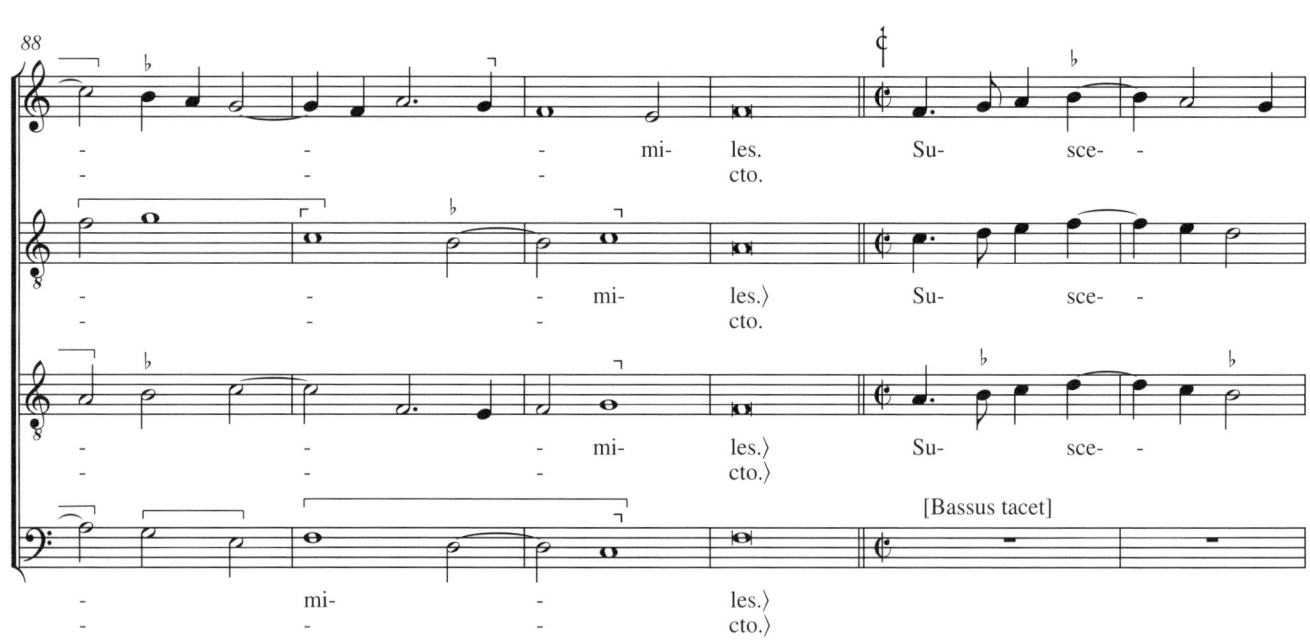
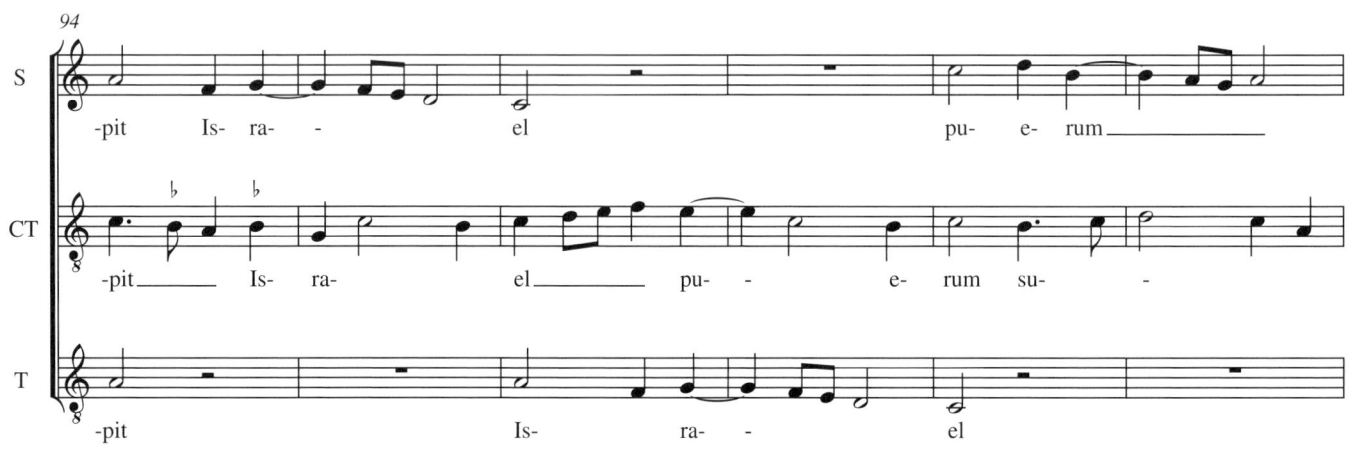

19. Magnificat 8. toni (1)

Johannes Martini

20. Magnificat 8. toni (2)

Johannes Martini

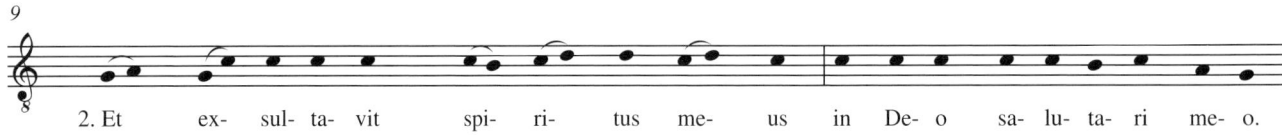

21. Magnificat 8. toni (3)

Johannes Martini

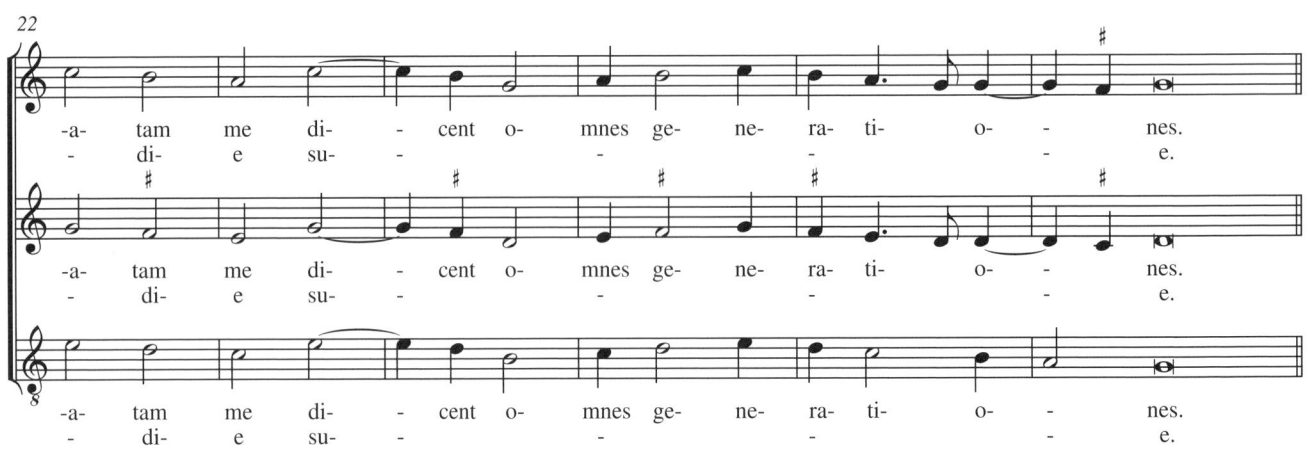

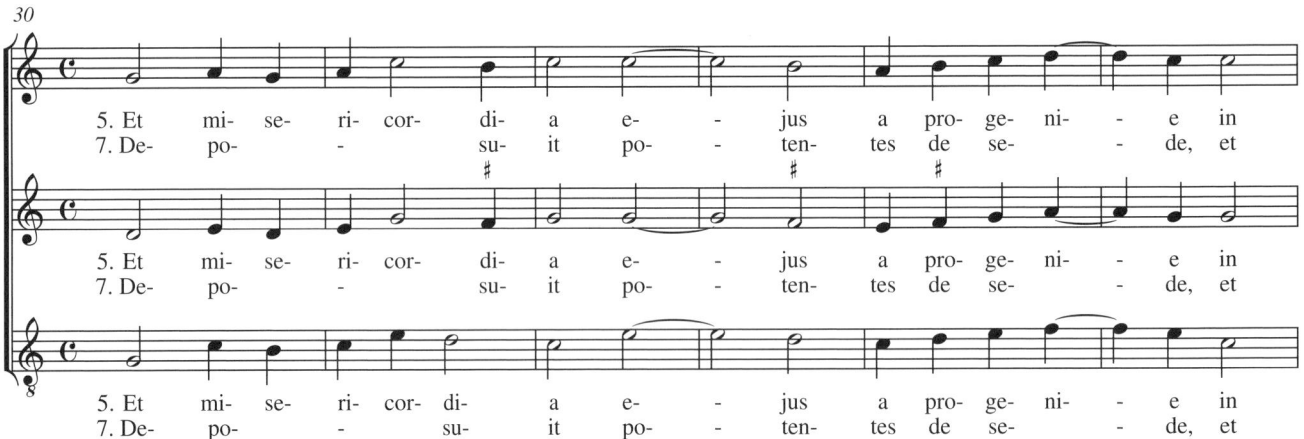

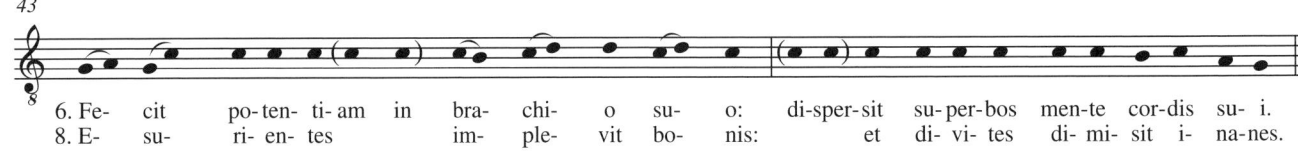

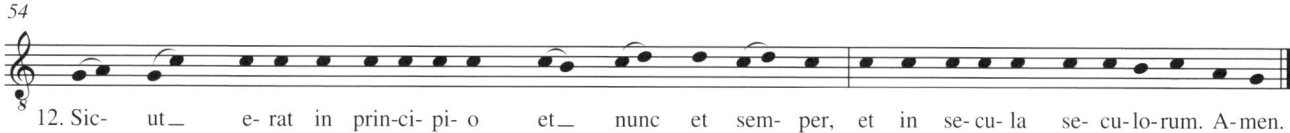

22. Ave decus virginale

Johannes Martini

22
-at ve- - ni- a- - - -
-at ⟨ve- ni- - a- - - le⟩ O-
Per te fi- at ve- ni-
te fi- at ve- ni- a- - -
28
-le O- mne quod com- mit- ti- - mus.
-mne quod ⟨com- mit- ti- - - mus.⟩
-a- le O- mne quod
-le O- mne quod com- mit- ti- - mus, ⟨o- - mne quod com-
34
Tu no- bis es sin- gu- la- -
Tu no- bis es sin- gu- la- - -
com- mit- ti- - mus. Tu no- bis
- mit- ti- mus.⟩ Tu no- bis es sin-

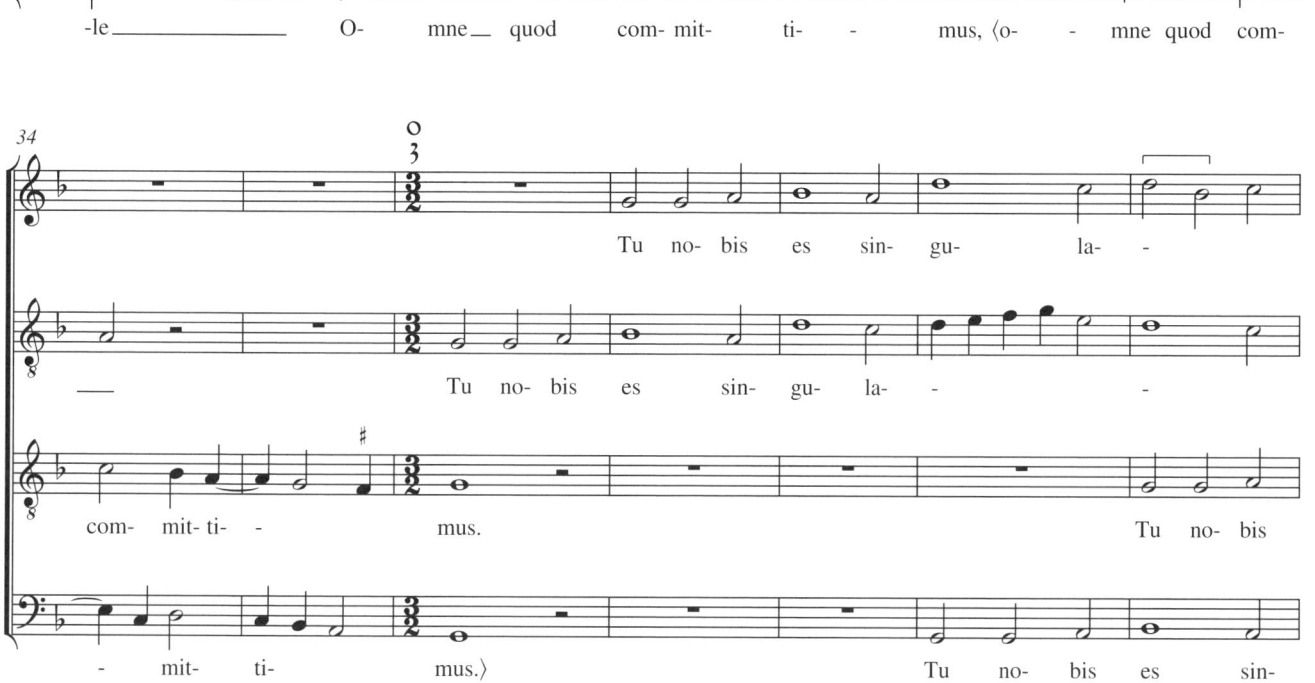

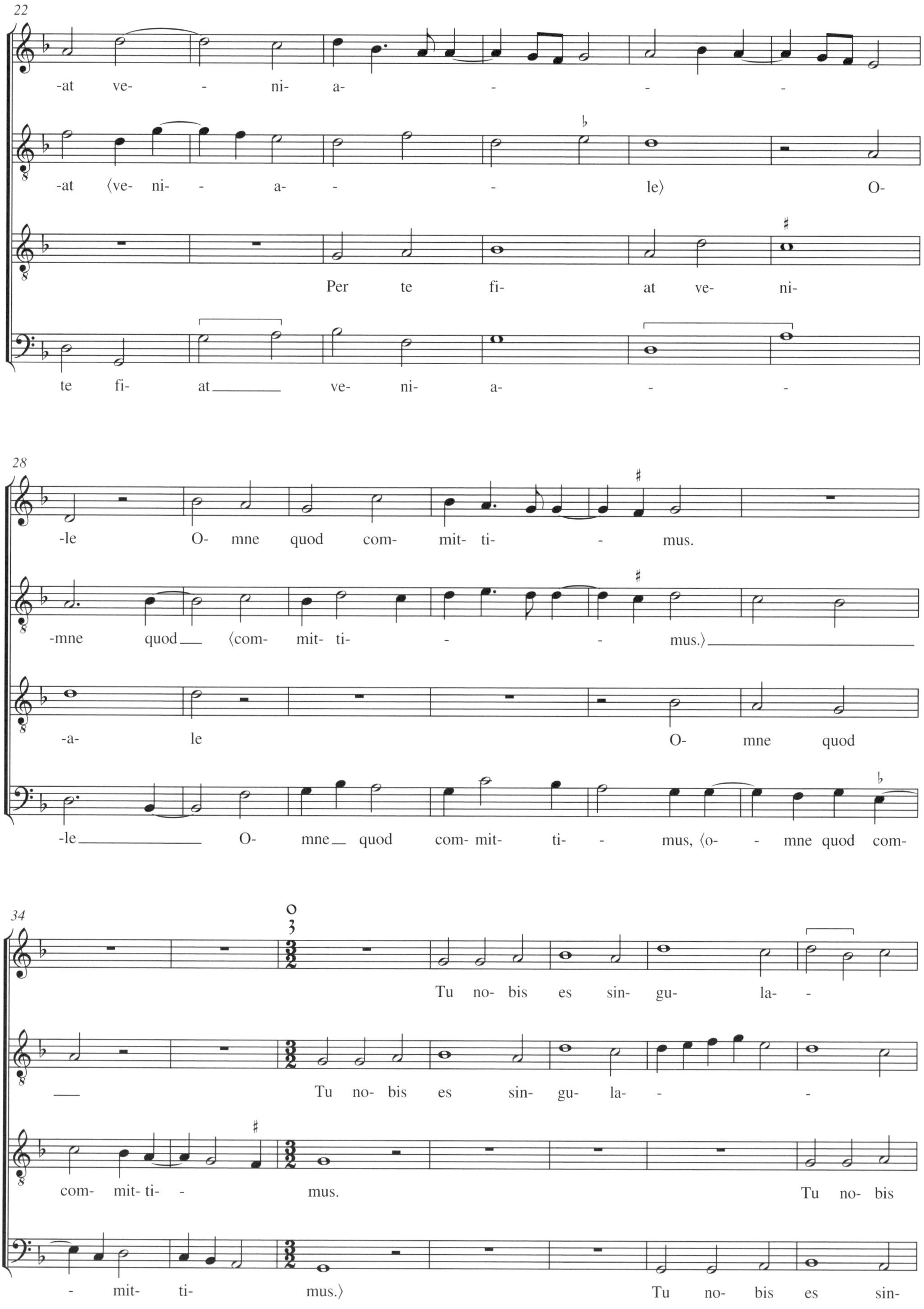

23. Da pacem, Domine

Johannes Martini

24. Domine, non secundum

Johannes Martini

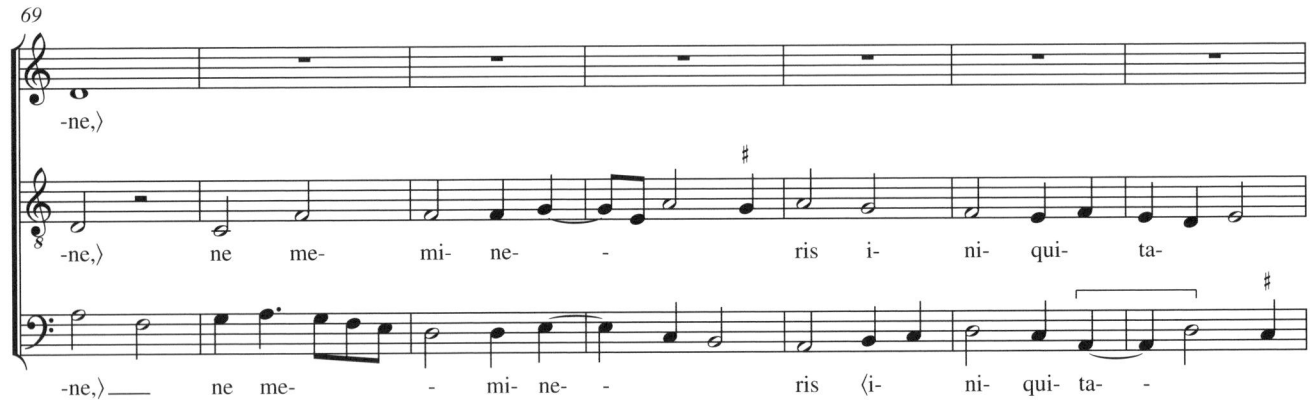

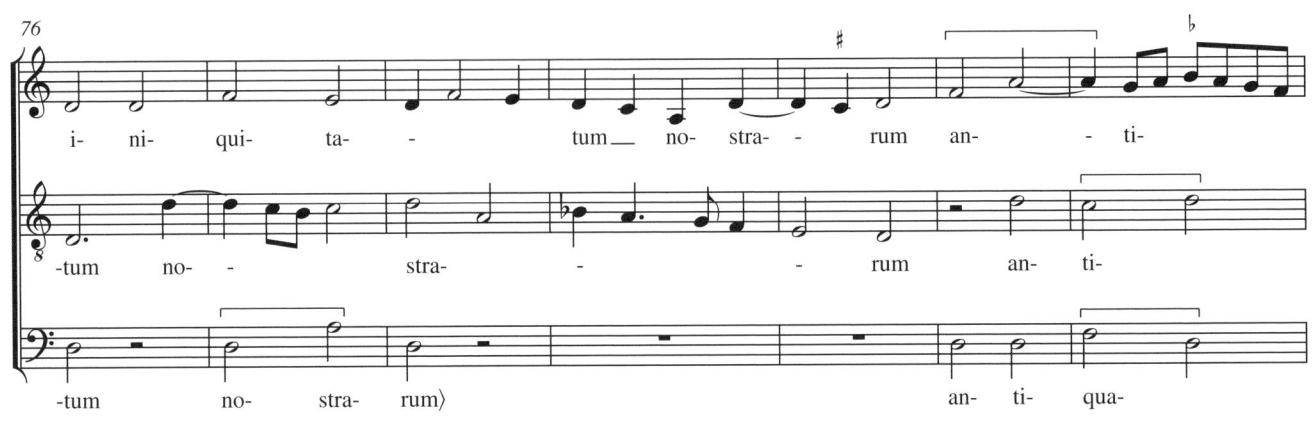

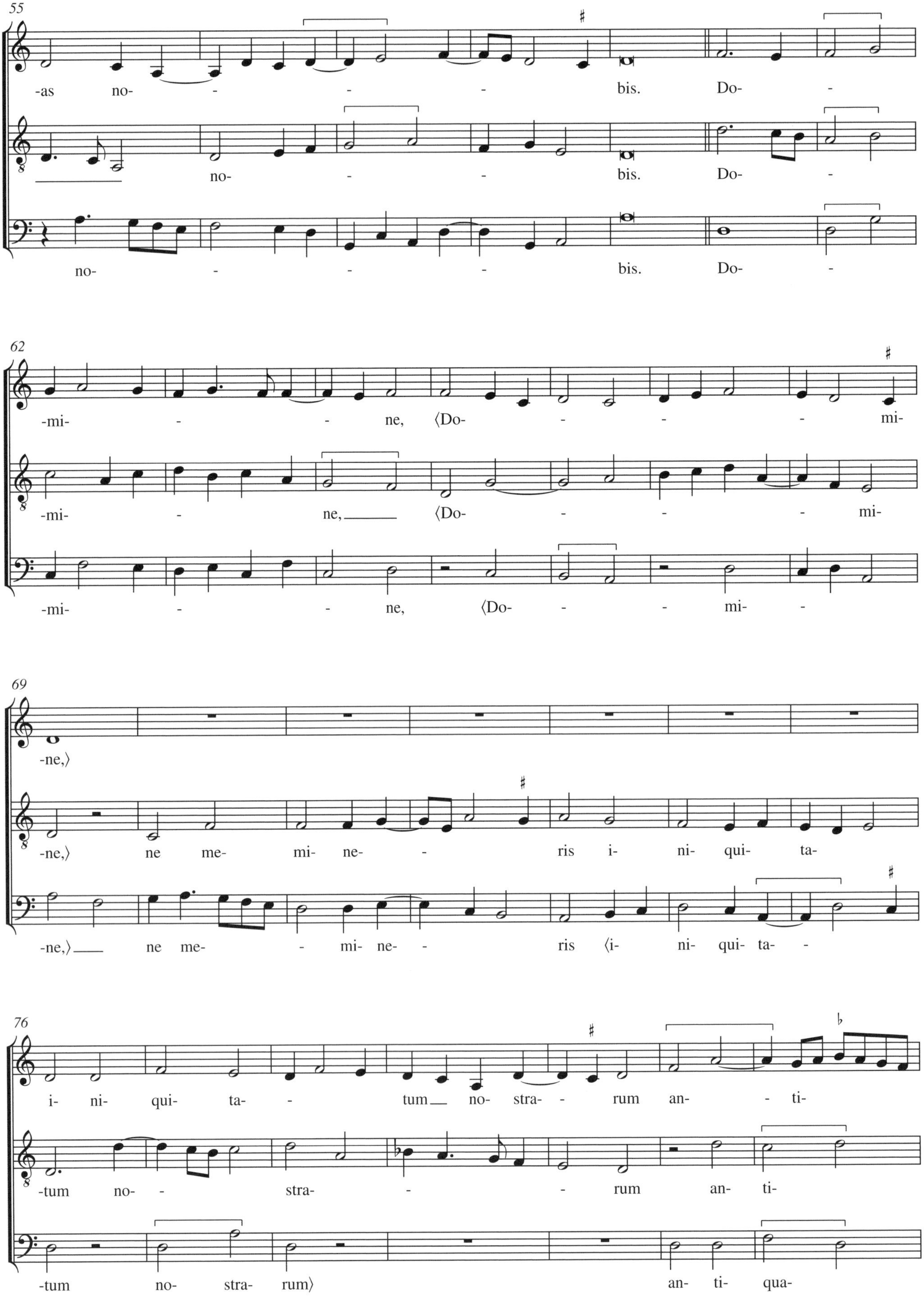
55
-as no- - - bis. Do- -
no- - - bis. Do- -
no- - - - bis. Do- -
62
-mi- - - ne, ⟨Do- - - - mi-
-mi- - ne, ⟨Do- - - mi-
-mi- - - ne, ⟨Do- - - mi- -
69
-ne,⟩
-ne,⟩ ne me- mi- ne- - ris i- ni- qui- ta-
-ne,⟩ ne me- - mi- ne- - ris ⟨i- ni- qui- ta- -
76
i- ni- qui- ta- - tum no- stra- - rum an- - ti-
-tum no- - stra- - - rum an- ti-
-tum no- stra- rum⟩ an- ti- qua-

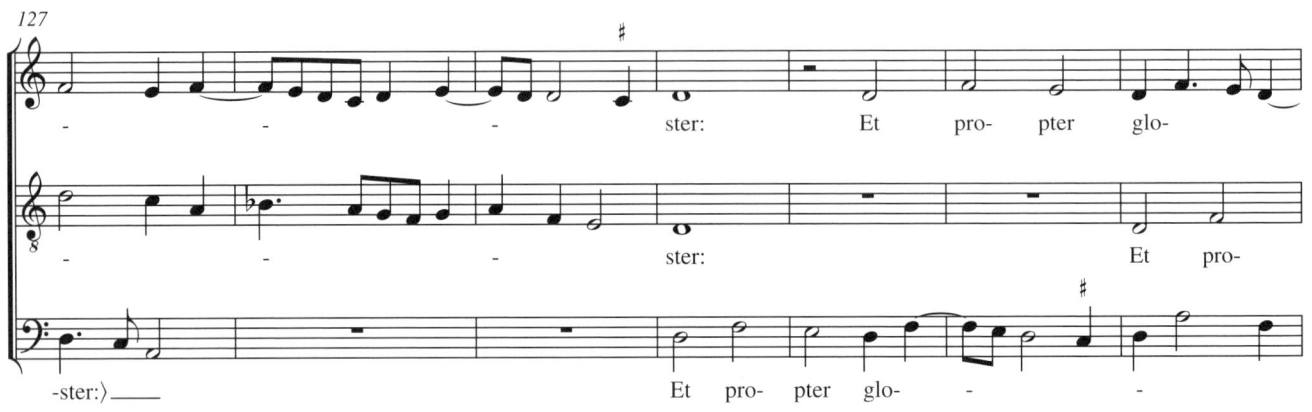

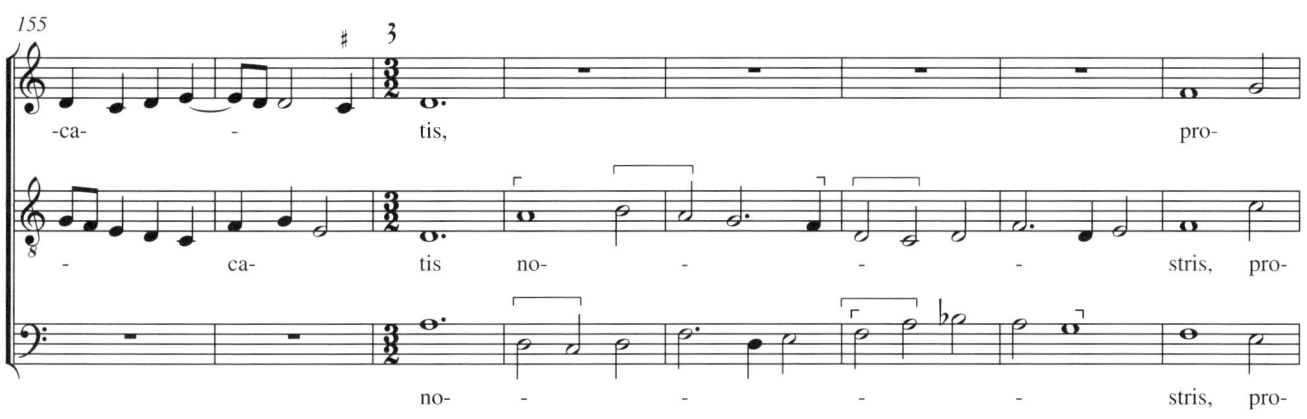

124

25. Levate capita vestra

Johannes Martini

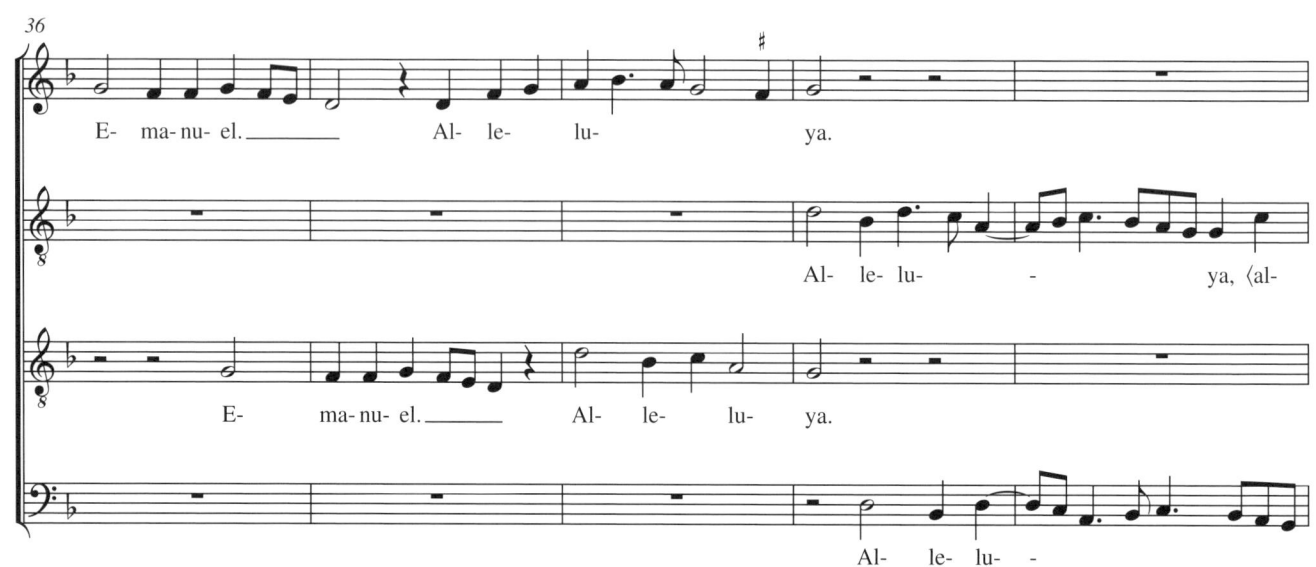

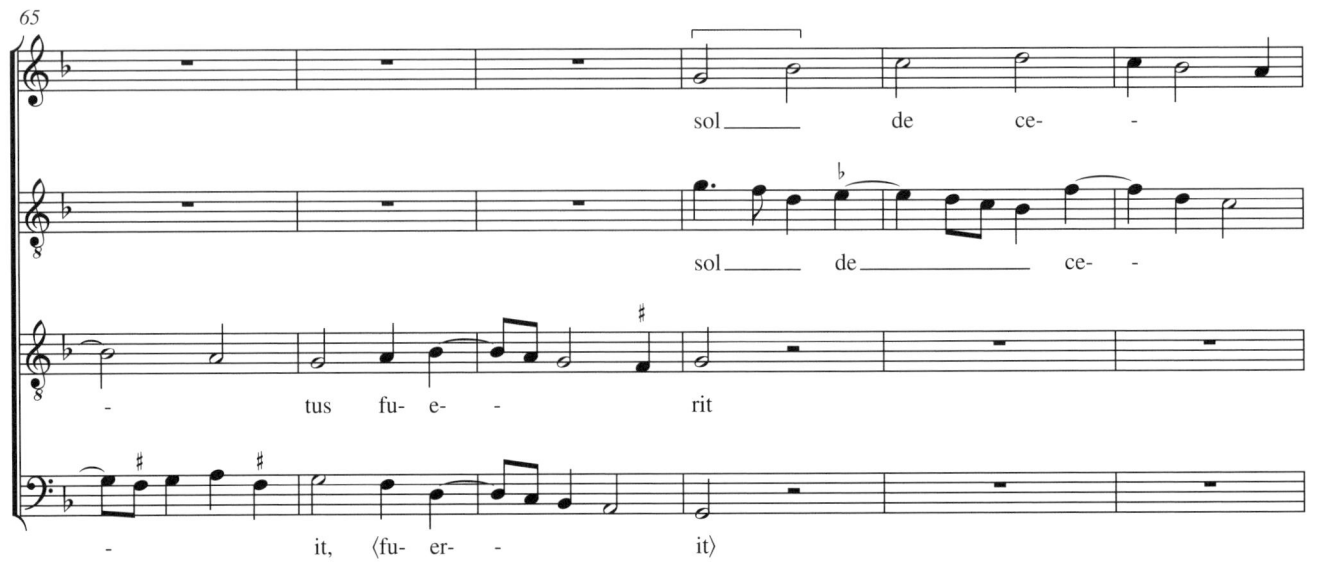

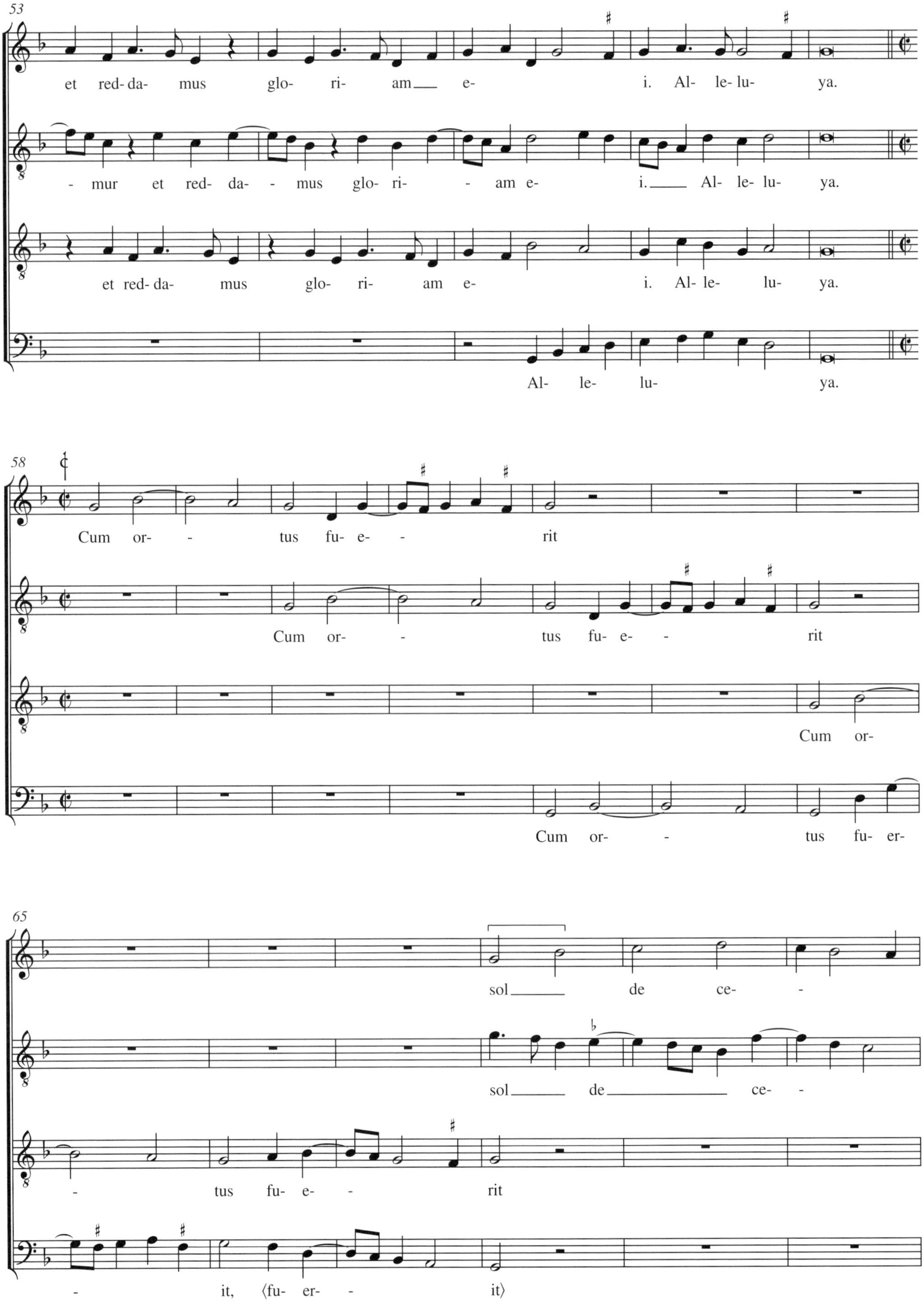
53
et red- da- mus glo- ri- am e- i. Al- le- lu- ya.
- mur et red- da- - mus glo- ri- - am e- i. Al- le- lu- ya.
et red- da- mus glo- ri- am e- i. Al- le- lu- ya.
Al- le- lu- ya.
58
Cum or- - tus fu- e- - rit
Cum or- - tus fu- e- - rit
Cum or-
Cum or- - tus fu- er-
65
sol de ce- -
sol de ce- -
- tus fu- e- - rit
- it, ⟨fu- er- - it⟩

130

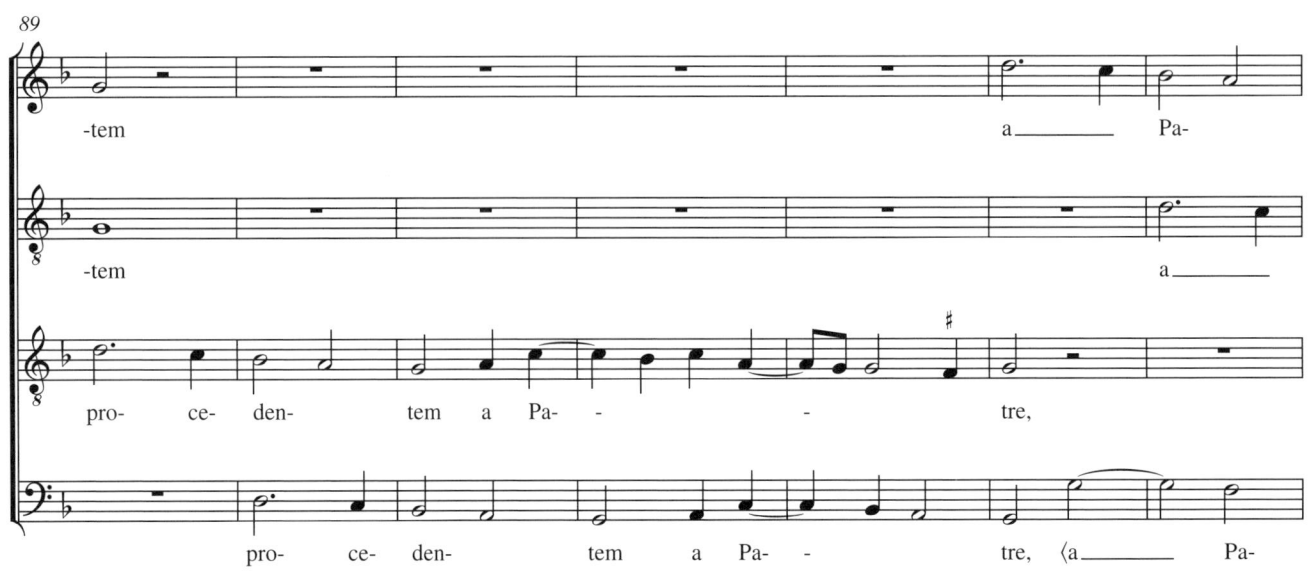

131

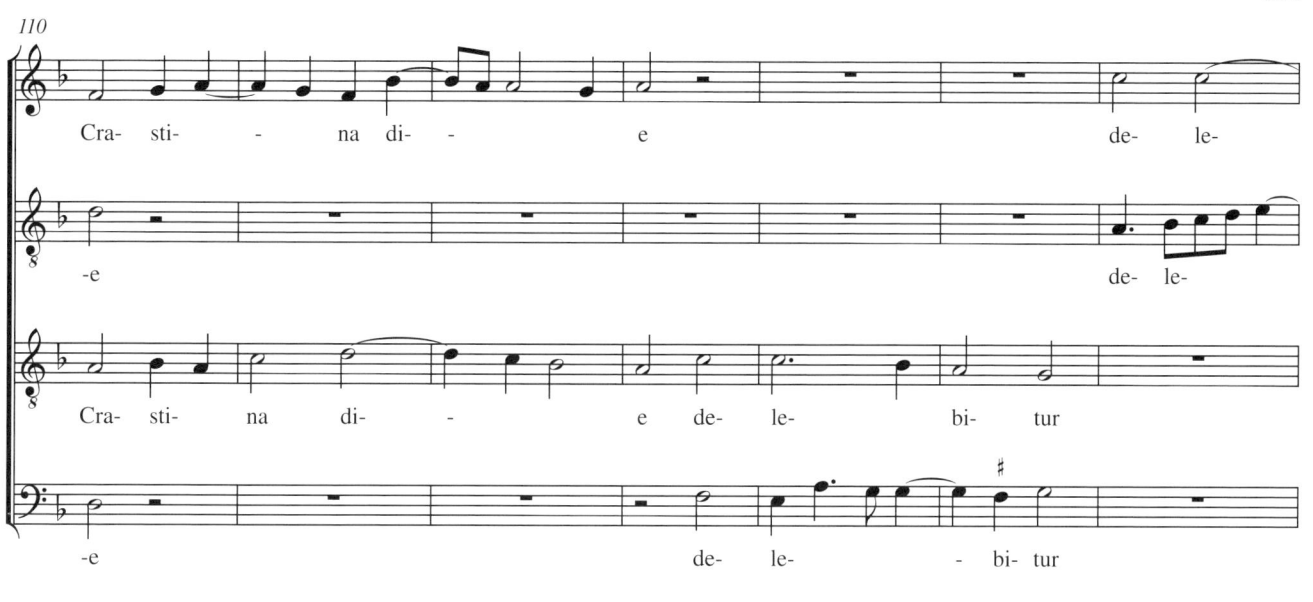

26. O beate Sebastiane

Johannes Martini

139

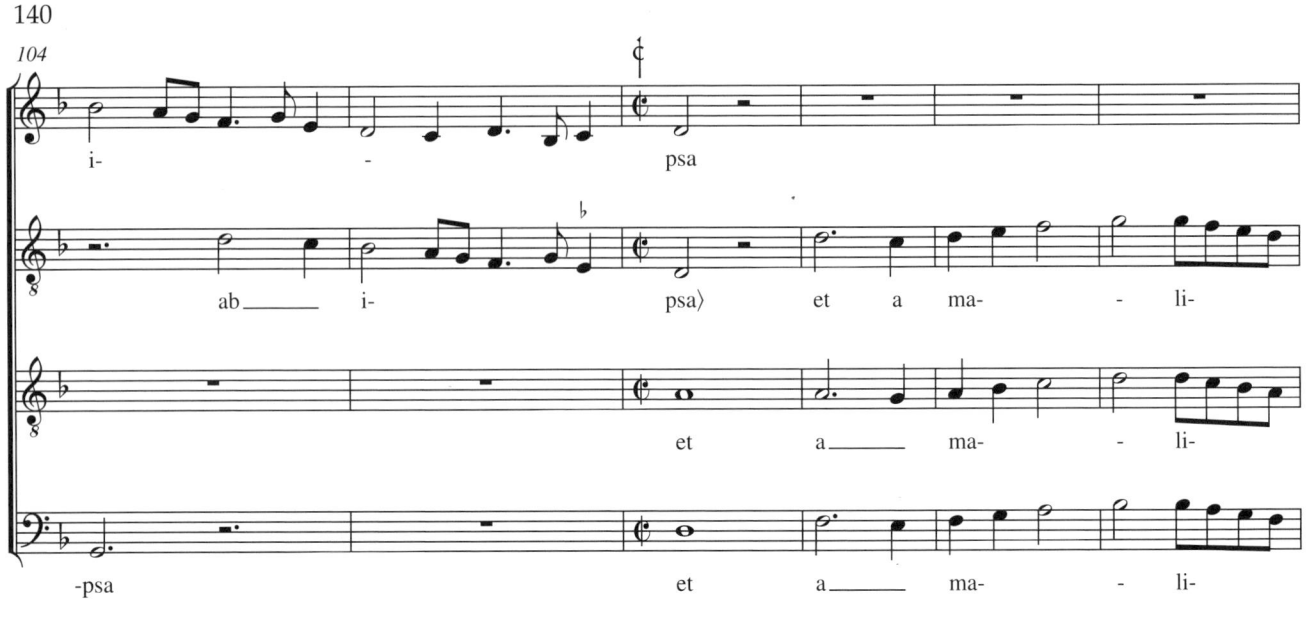
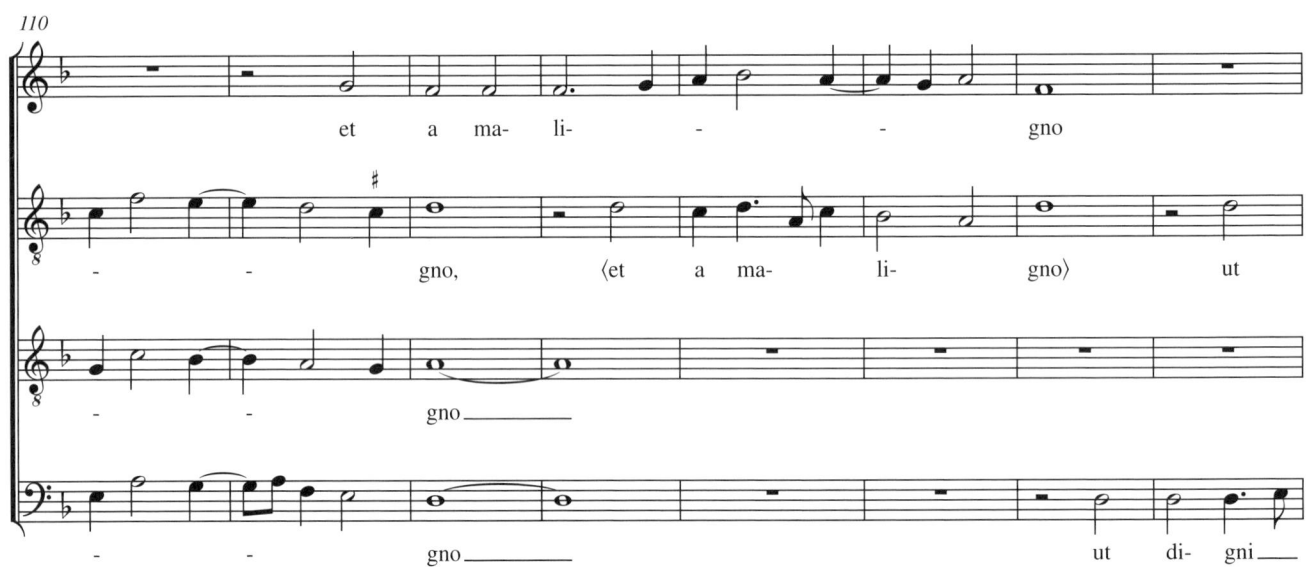

27. Jesum Nazarenum

John, chaps. 18–19　　　　　　　　　　　　　　　　　　　　　　　　　　Johannes Martini

147

28. Non in die festo

Matthew, chaps. 26–27

Johannes Martini

39
un- guen- tum i- stud ve- nun- da- ri mul- to,
un- guen- tum i- stud ve- nun- da- ri mul- to,
un- guen- tum i- - stud ve- nun- da- ri mul- to,
un- guen- tum i- stud ve- nun- da- ri mul- to,
un- guen- tum i- stud ve- - nun- da- ri mul- to,
un- guen- tum i- stud ve- nun- da- ri mul- to,
48
et da- ri pau- pe- ri- bus.
et da- ri pau- pe- - ri- bus.
et da- ri pau- pe- ri- - - bus.
et da- ri pau- pe- ri- bus.
et da- ri pau- pe- ri- - bus.
et da- ri pau- - pe- ri- - bus.

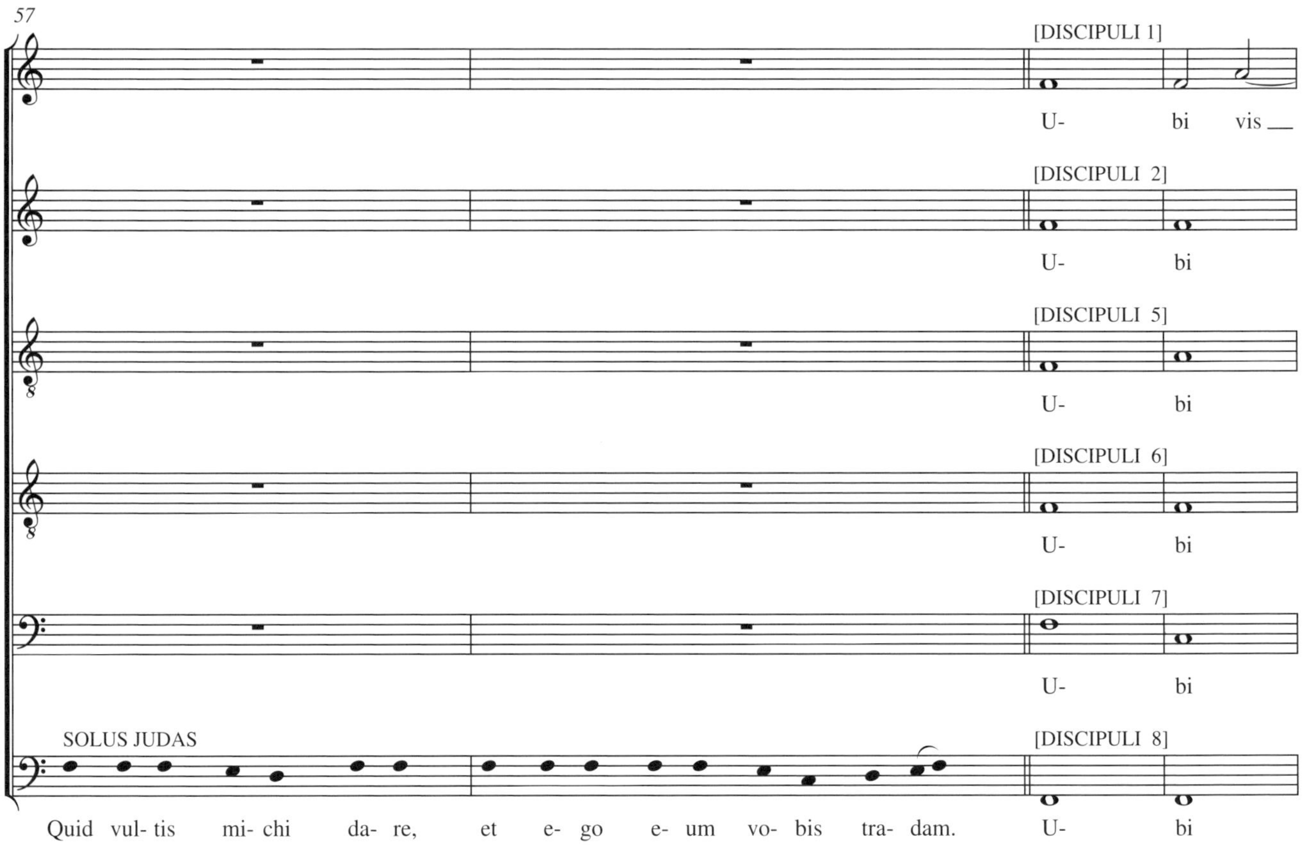
57
[DISCIPULI 1]
U- bi vis
[DISCIPULI 2]
U- bi
[DISCIPULI 5]
U- bi
[DISCIPULI 6]
U- bi
[DISCIPULI 7]
U- bi
SOLUS JUDAS
[DISCIPULI 8]
Quid vul- tis mi- chi da- re, et e- go e- um vo- bis tra- dam.
U- bi

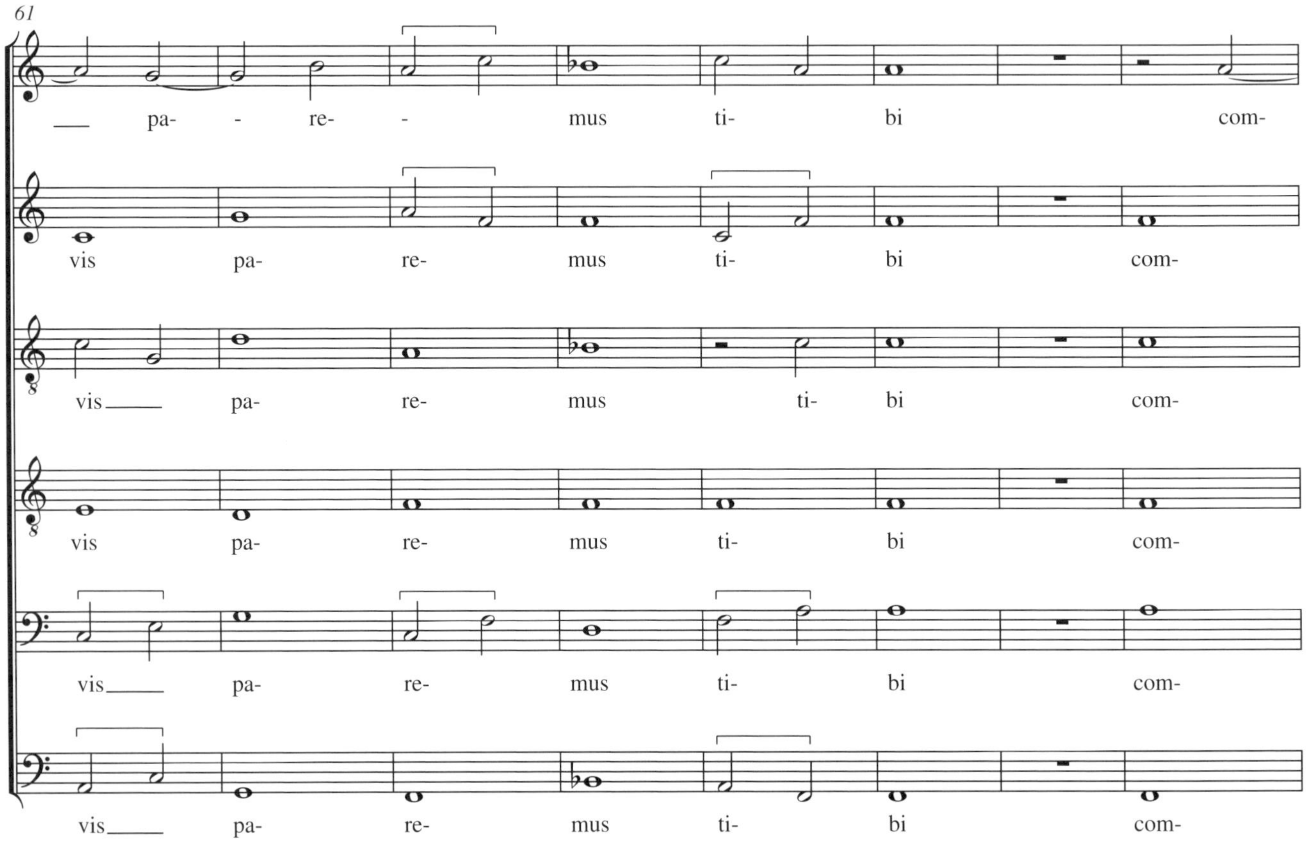
61
pa- - re- - mus ti- bi com-
vis pa- re- mus ti- bi com-
vis pa- re- mus ti- bi com-
vis pa- re- mus ti- bi com-
vis pa- re- mus ti- bi com-
vis pa- re- mus ti- bi com-

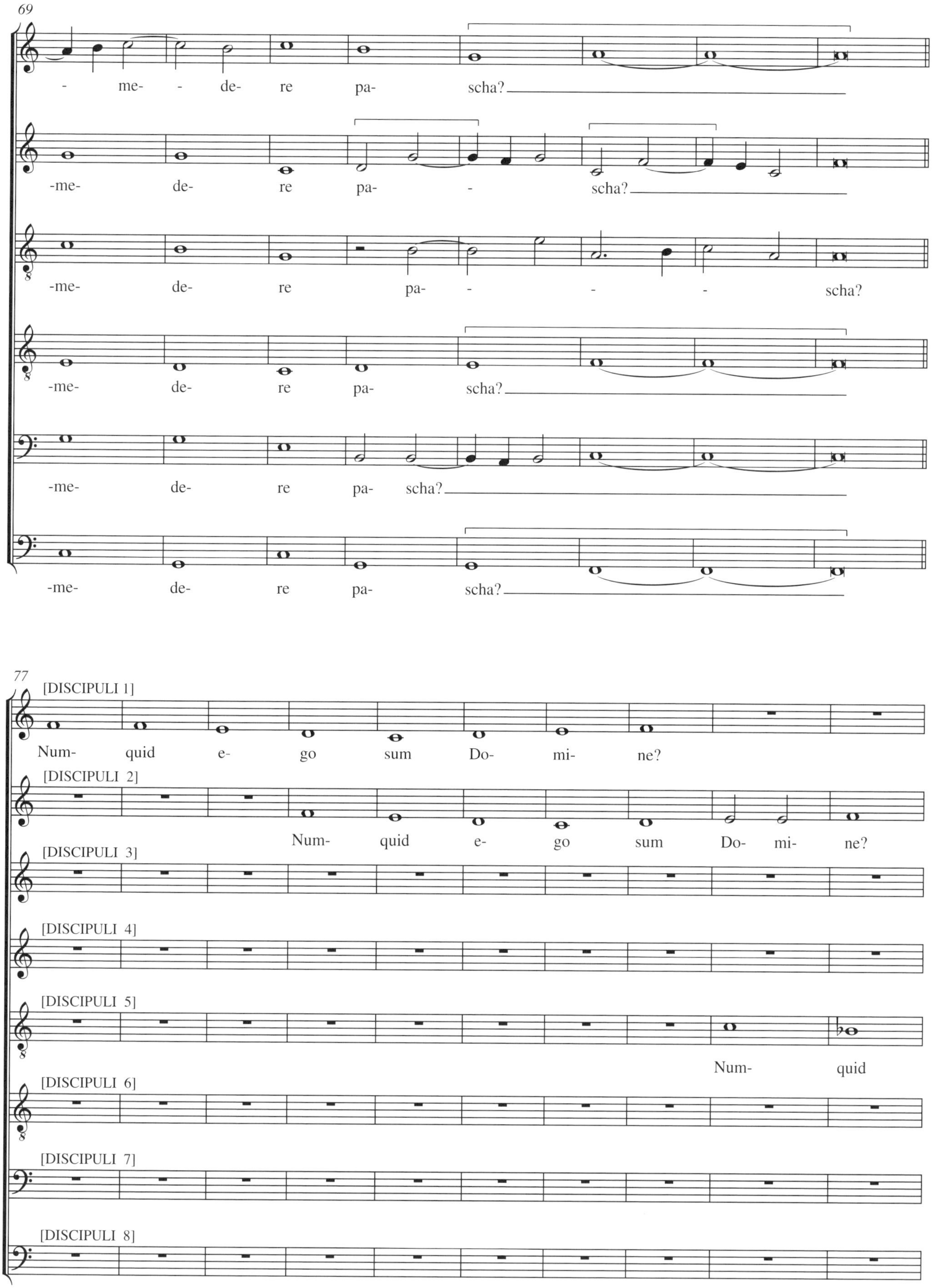

151

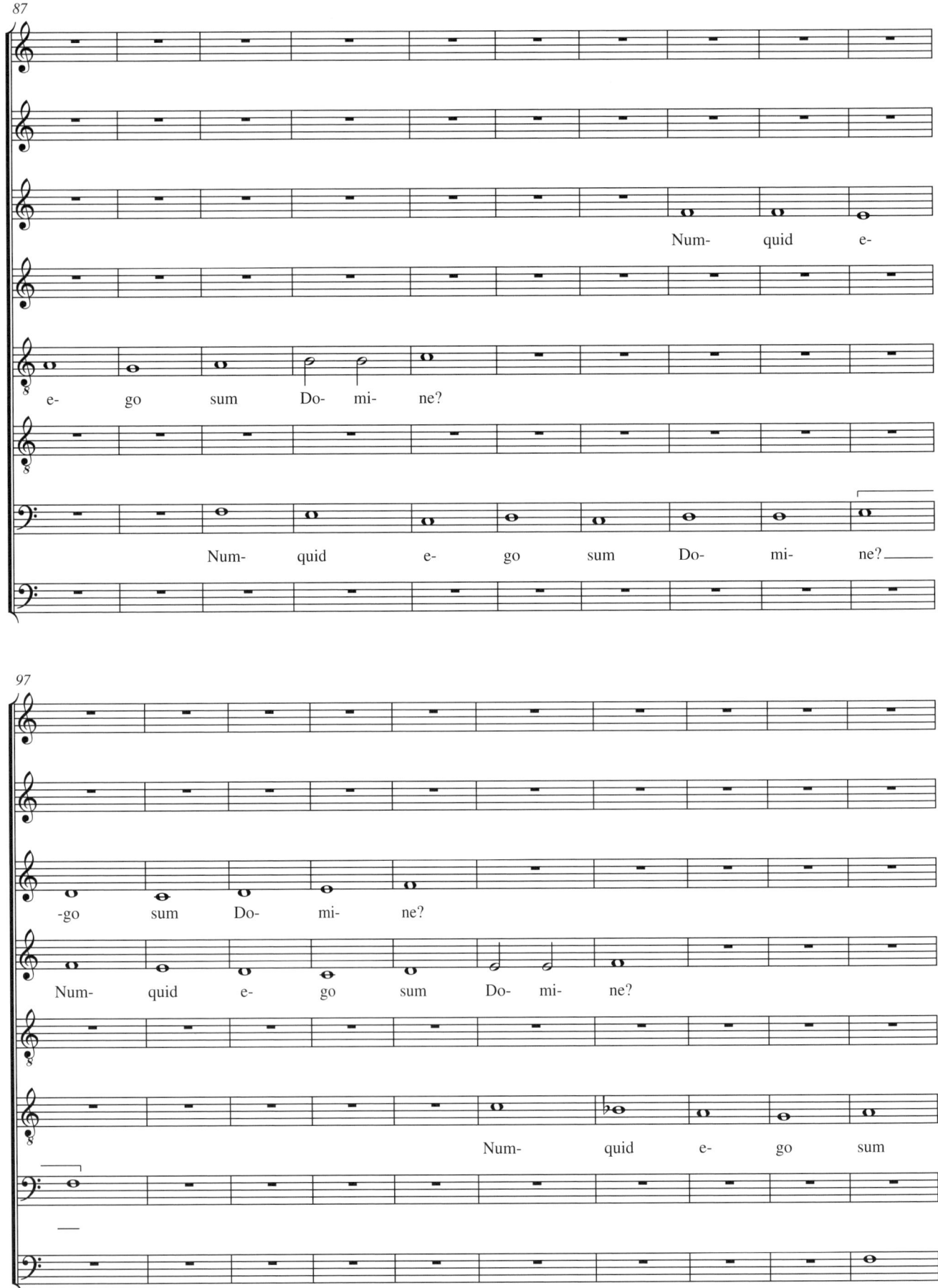

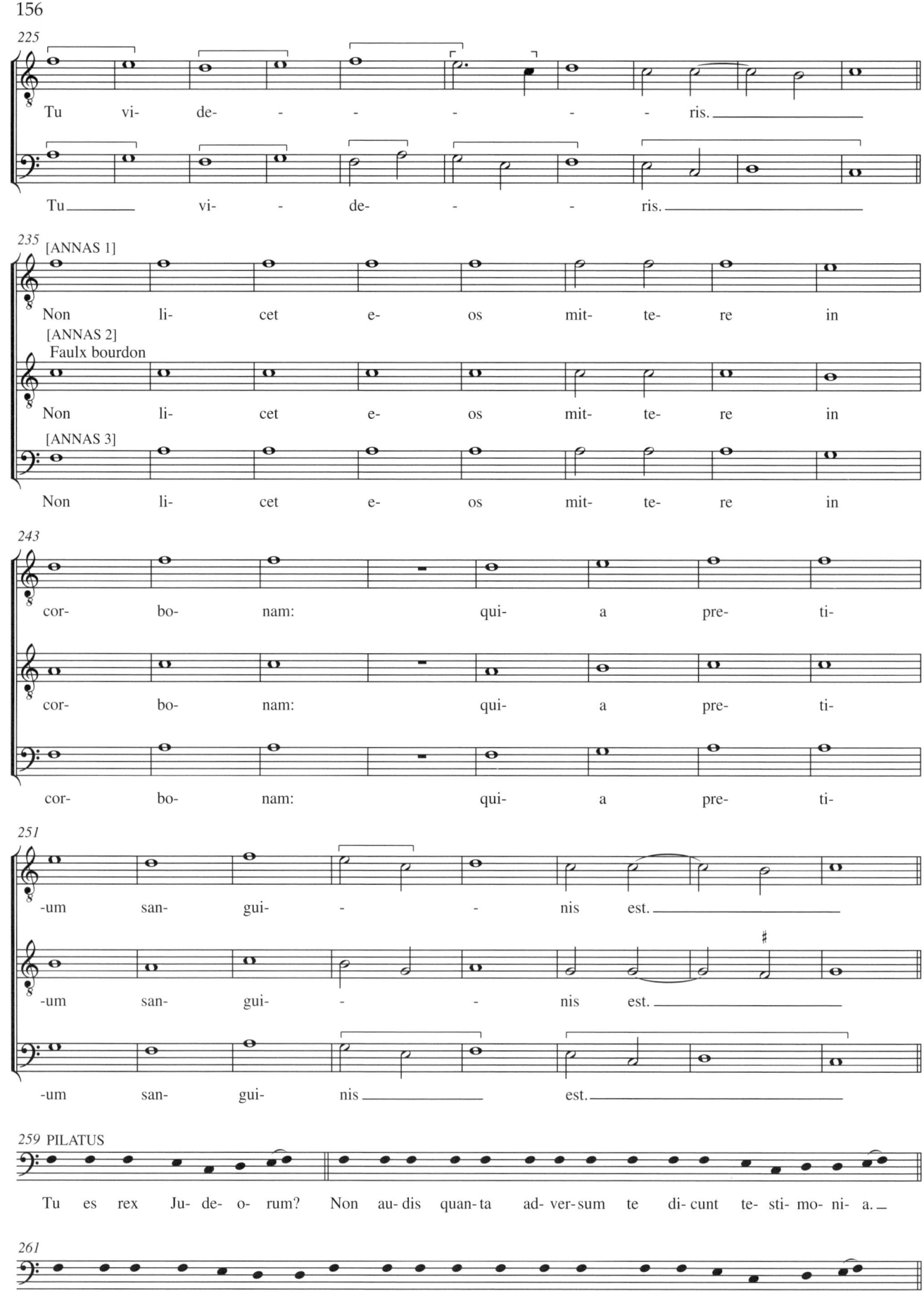

160

29. Perfunde celi rore

Johannes Martini

[Secunda pars]

166

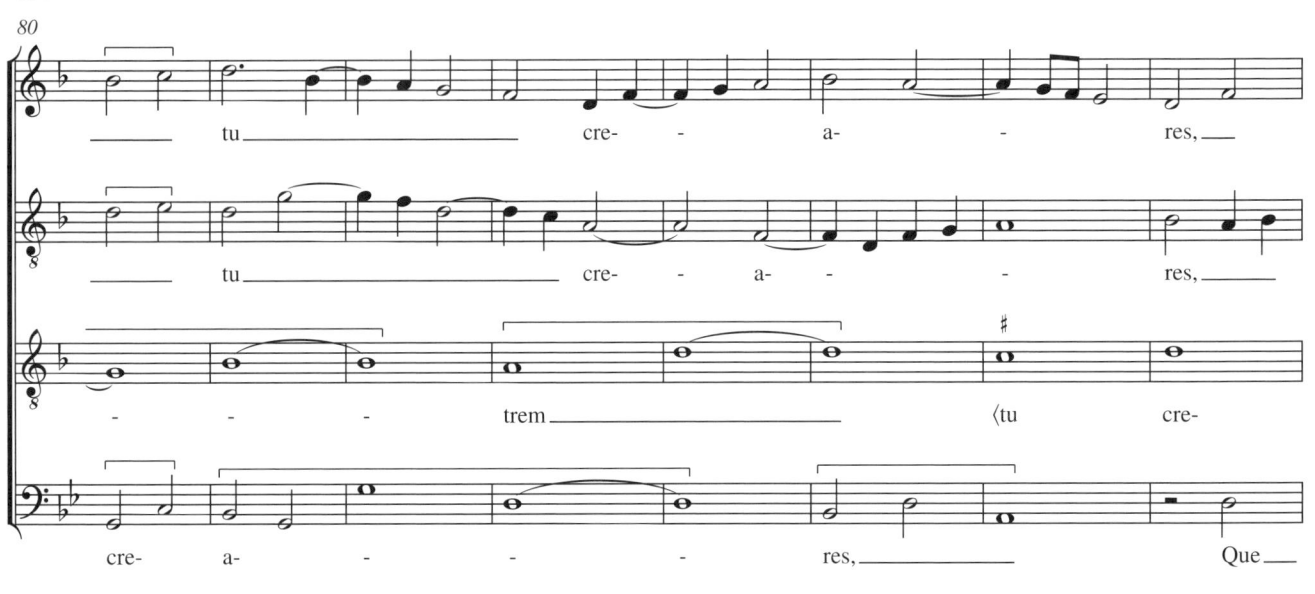
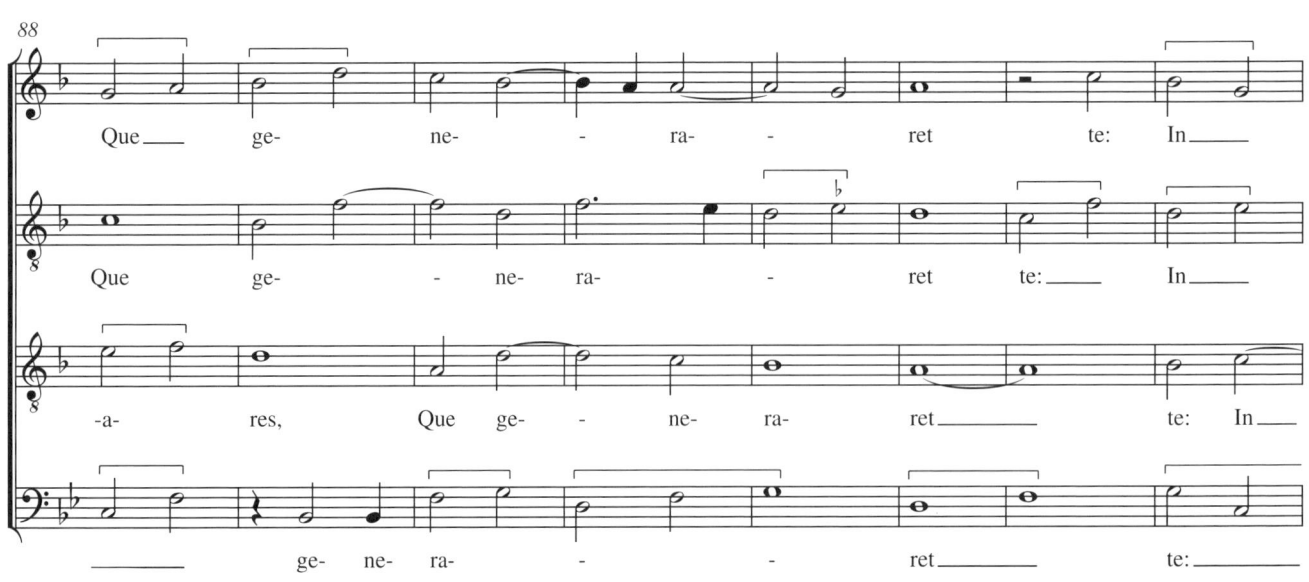

30. Hercules omni memorandus evo

Johannes Brebis

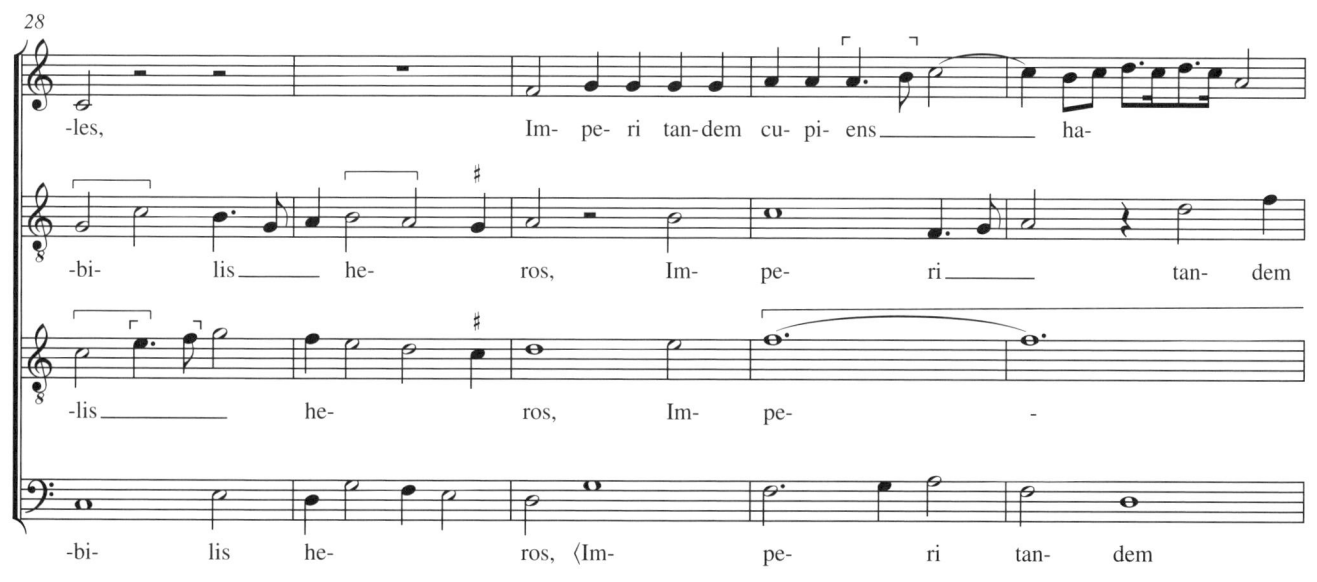

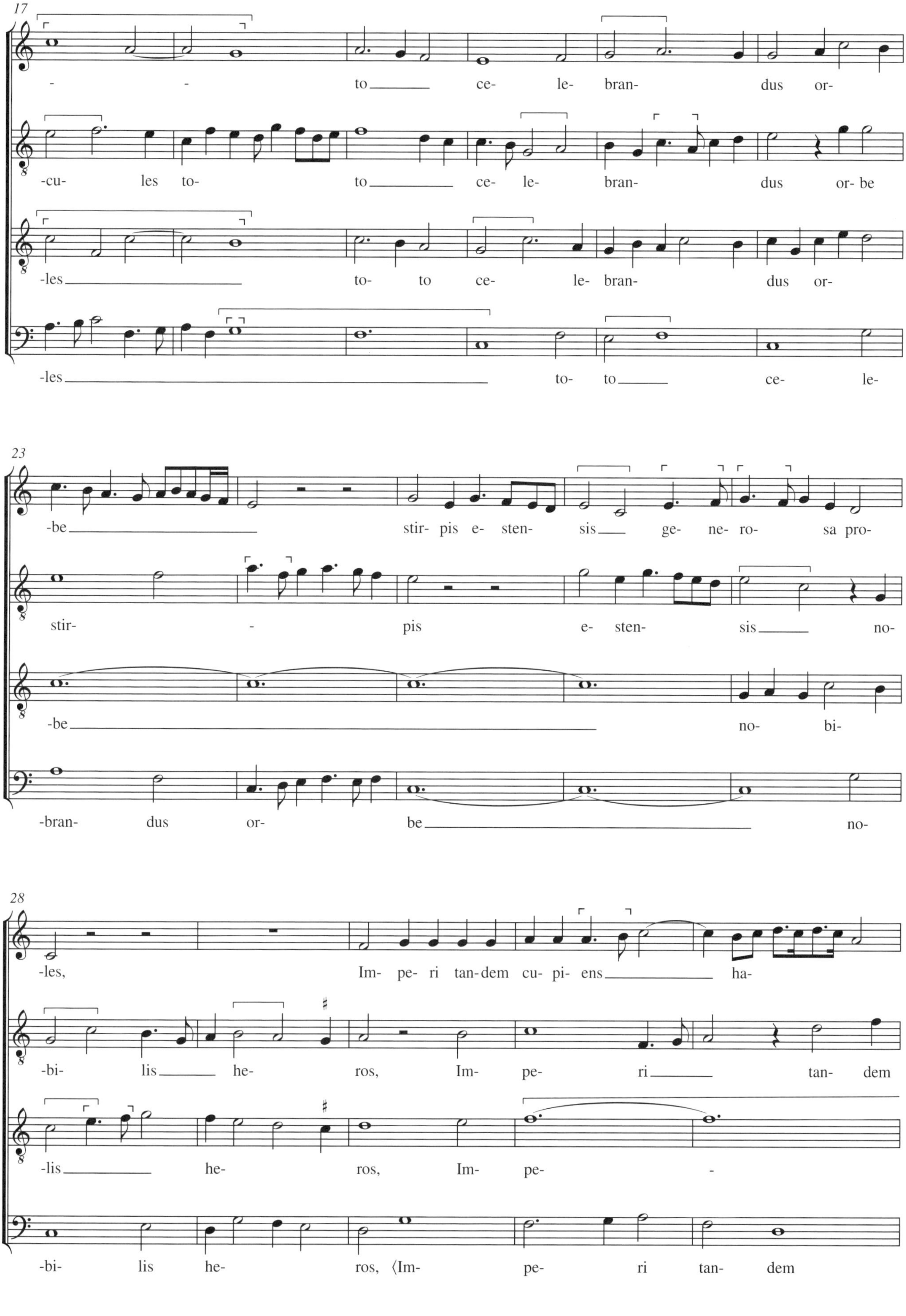
17
- - to ce- le- bran- dus or-
-cu- les to- to ce- le- bran- dus or- be
-les to- to ce- le- bran- dus or-
-les to- to ce- le-
23
-be stir- pis e- sten- sis ge- ne- ro- sa pro-
stir- - pis e- sten- sis no-
-be no- bi-
-bran- dus or- be no-
28
-les, Im- pe- ri tan- dem cu- pi- ens ha-
-bi- lis he- ros, Im- pe- ri tan- dem
-lis he- ros, Im- pe- -
-bi- lis he- ros, ⟨Im- pe- ri tan- dem

176

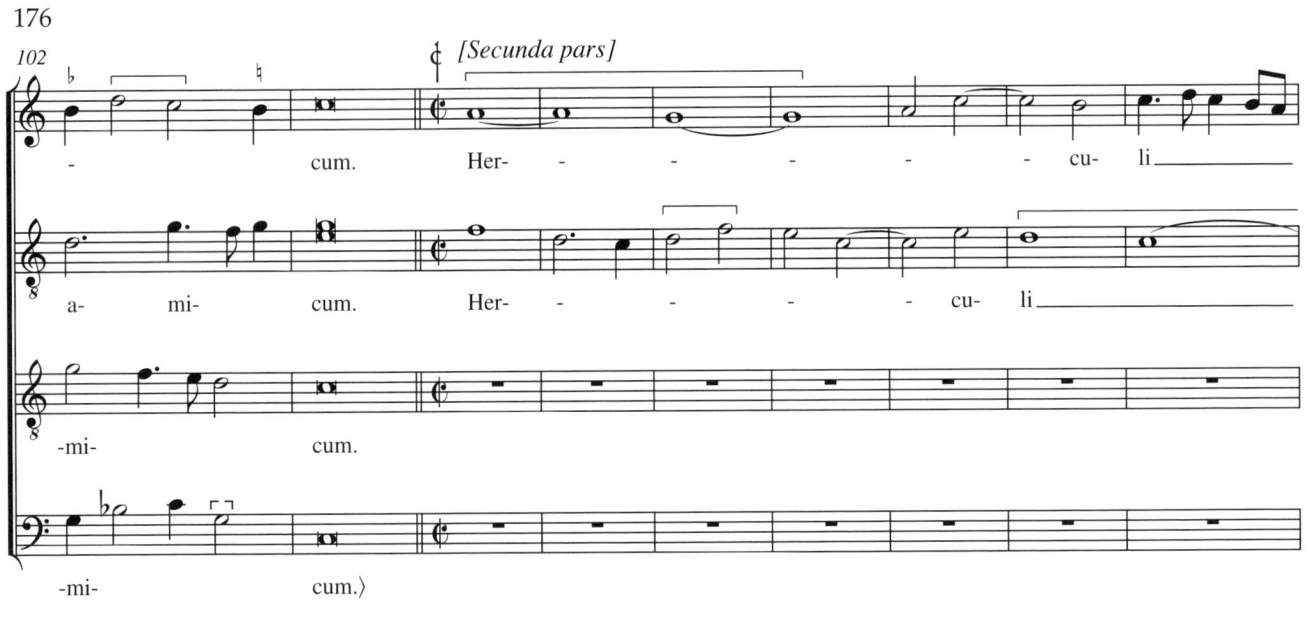

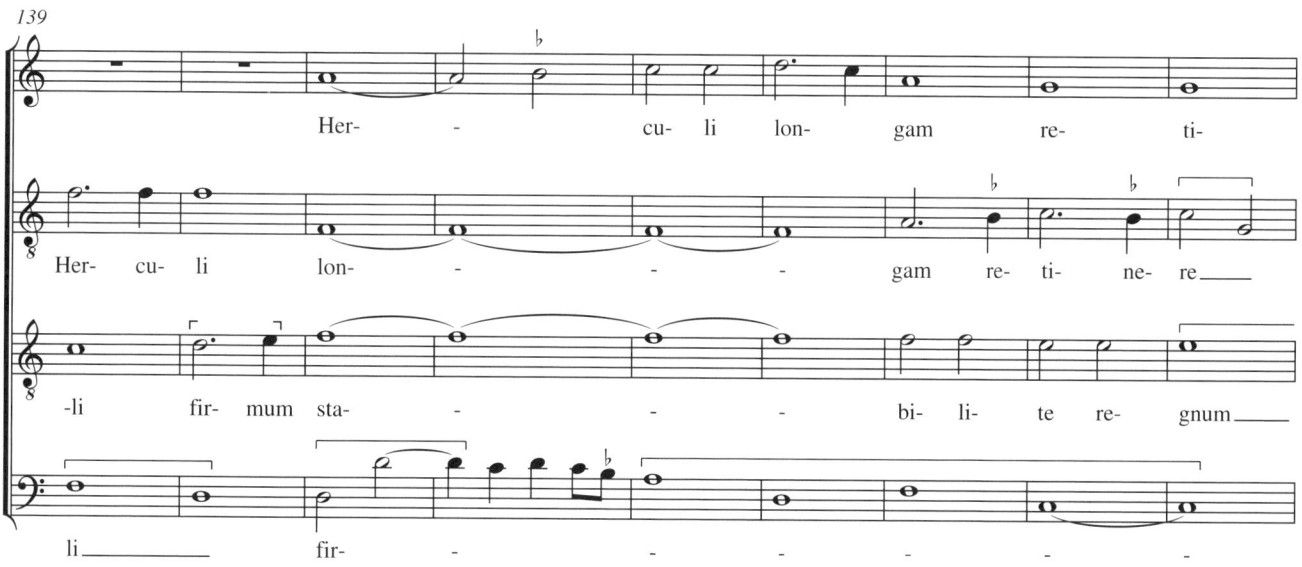

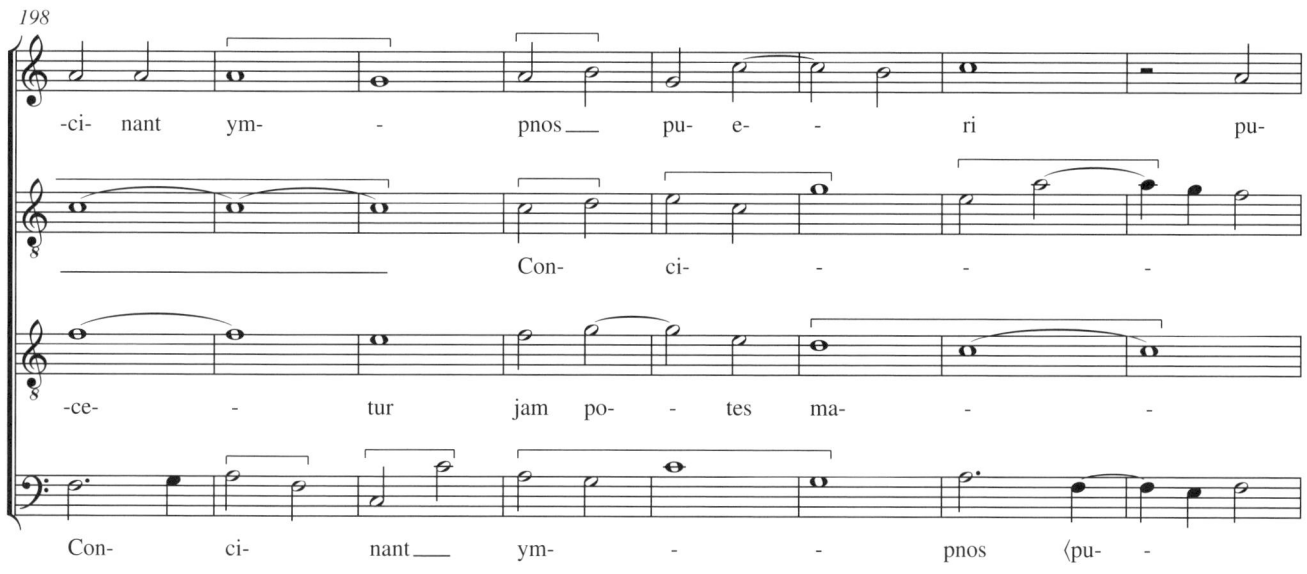

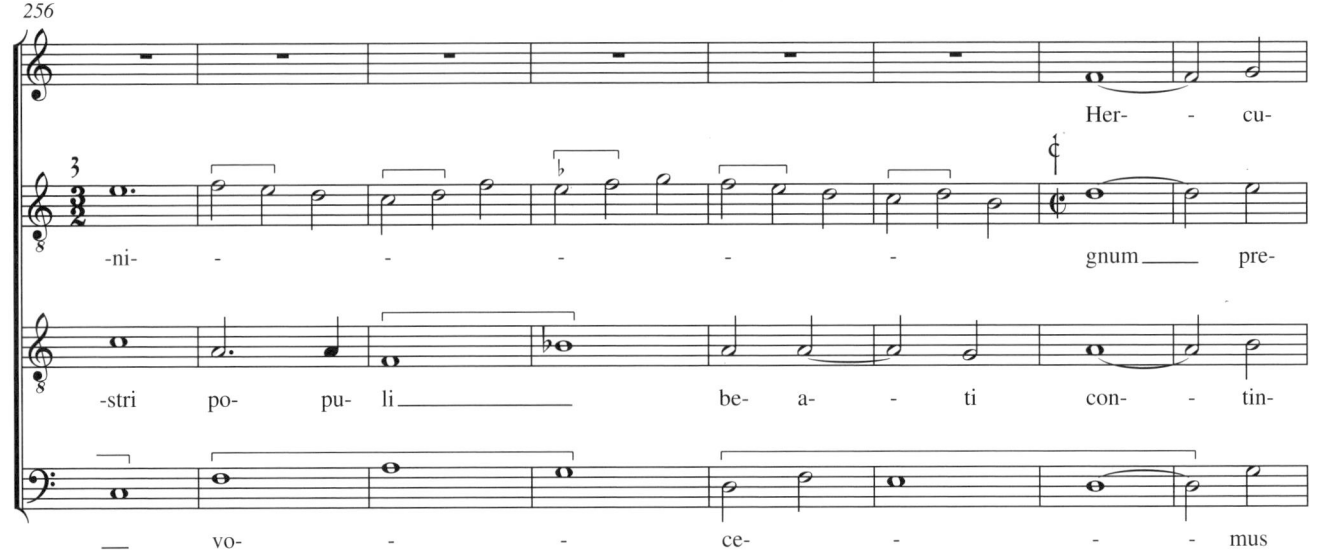

31. Salve Regina

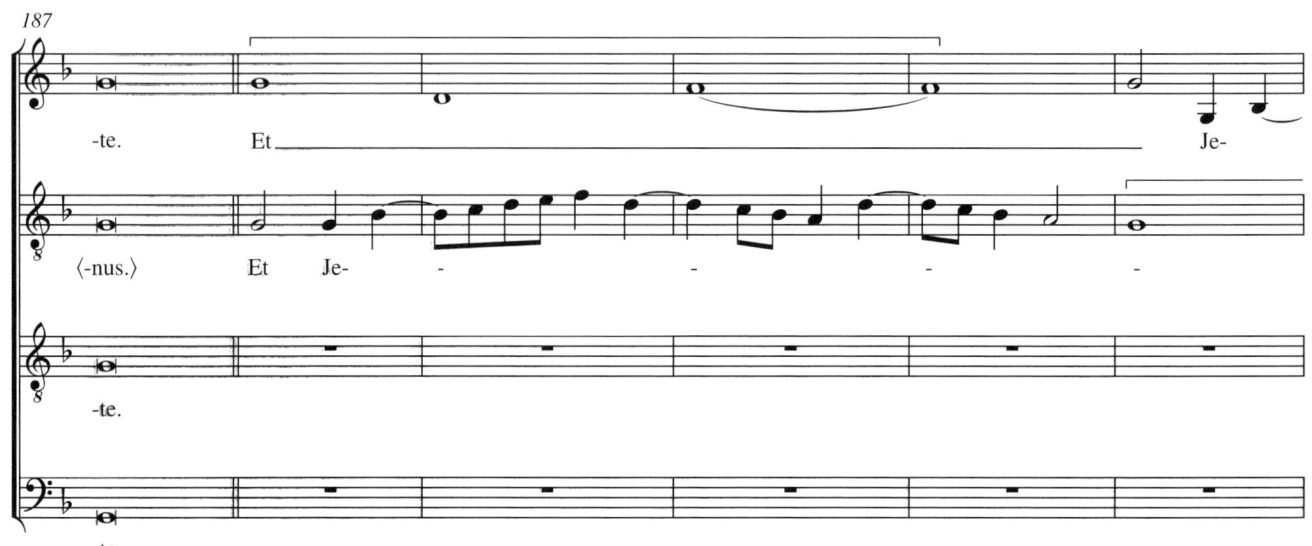

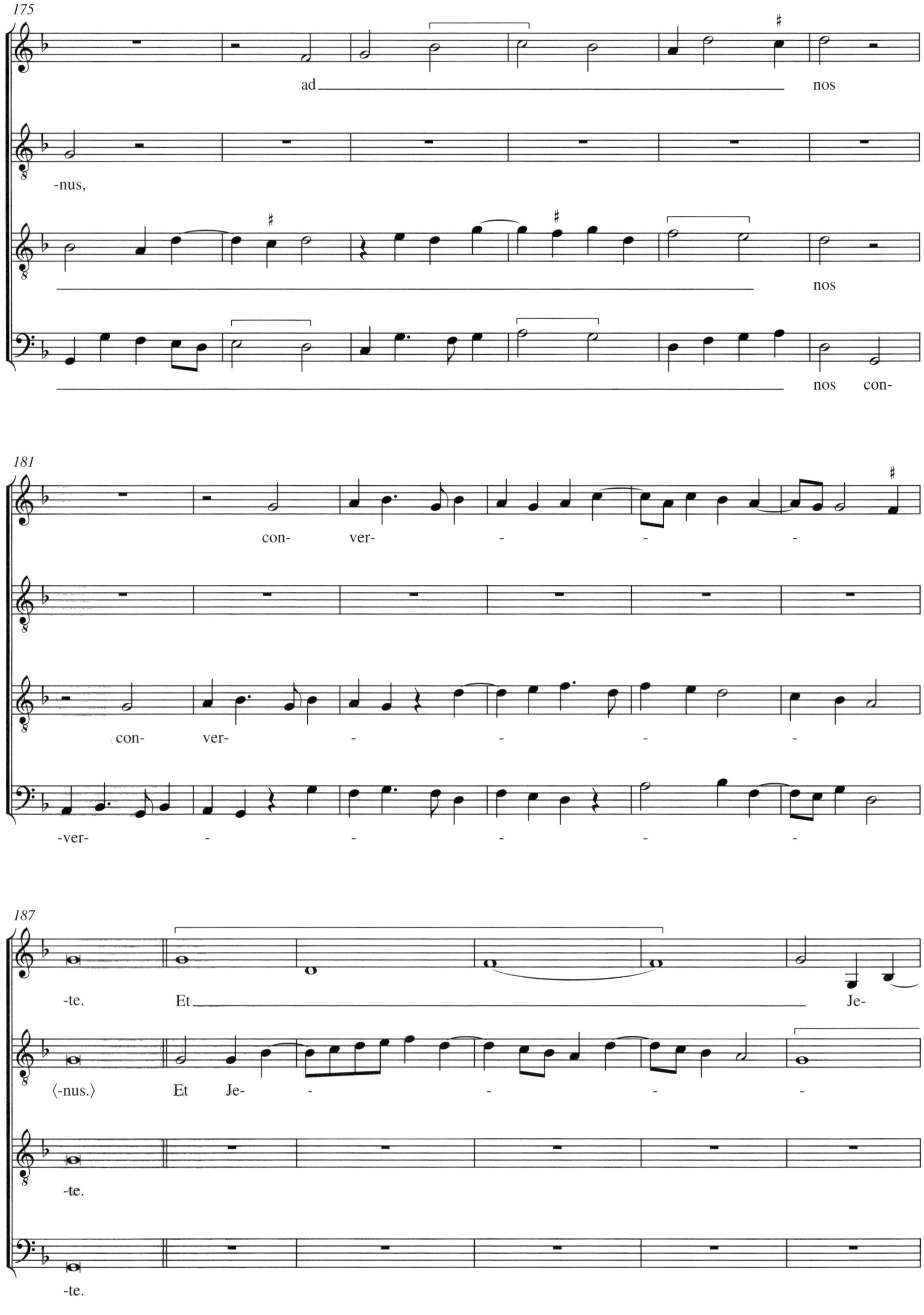
175
ad nos
-nus,
nos
nos con-
181
con- ver- - - -
con- ver- - - - -
-ver- - - - - -
187
-te. Et Je-
⟨-nus.⟩ Et Je- - - - -
-te.
-te.

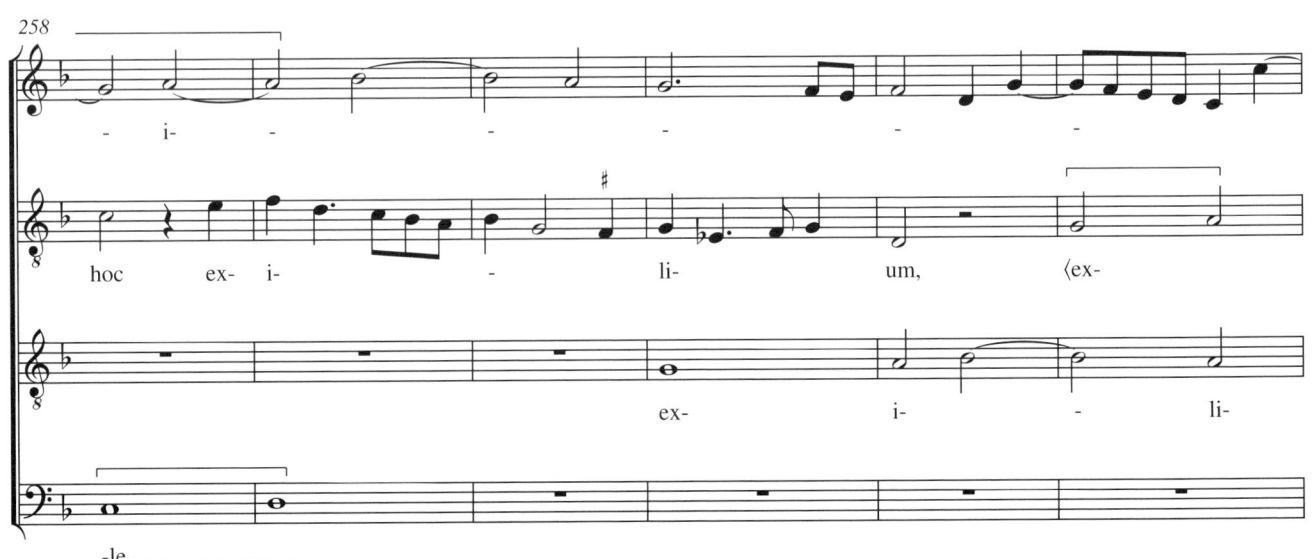

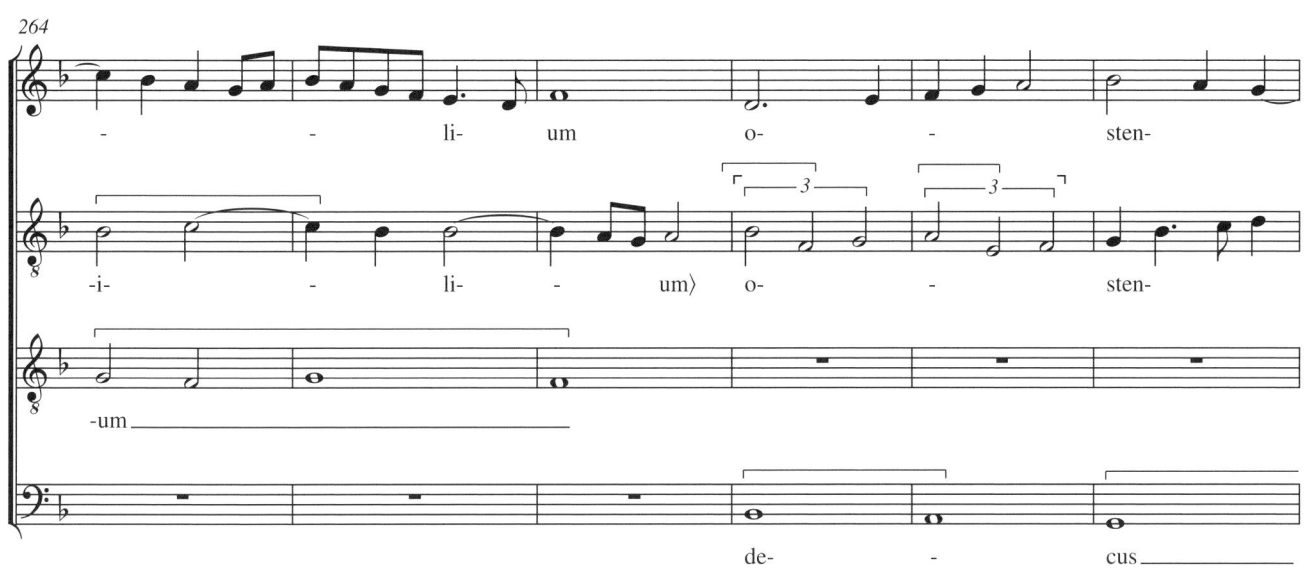

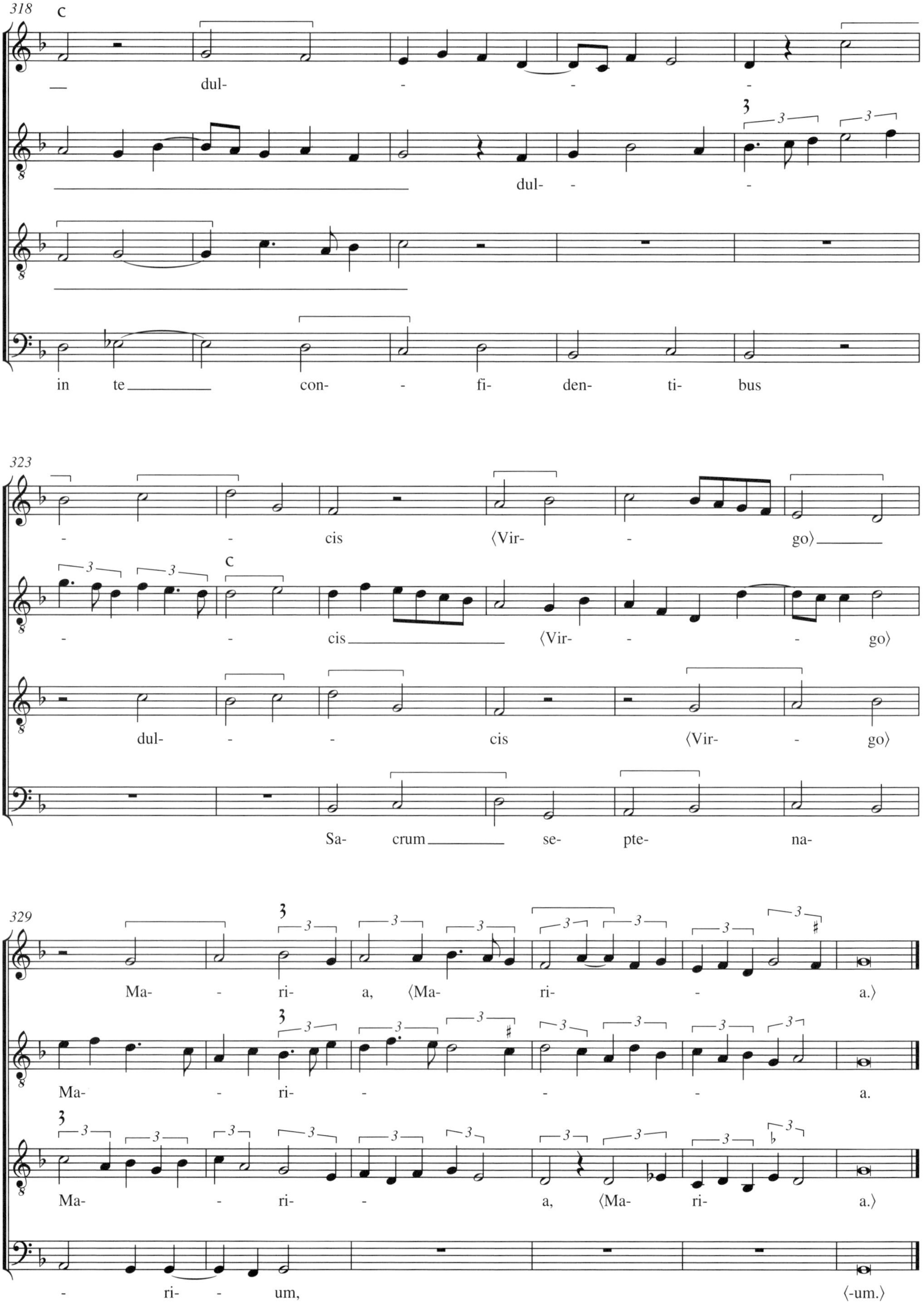
318
C
— dul- - - - -
dul- - -
in te con- - fi- den- ti- bus
323
C
- - cis ⟨Vir- - go⟩
- - cis ⟨Vir- - - go⟩
dul- - - cis ⟨Vir- - go⟩
Sa- crum se- pte- na-
329
Ma- - ri- a, ⟨Ma- ri- - a.⟩
Ma- - ri- - - - a.
Ma- - ri- - a, ⟨Ma- ri- a.⟩
- ri- - um, ⟨-um.⟩

RECENT RESEARCHES IN THE MUSIC OF THE MIDDLE AGES
AND EARLY RENAISSANCE
Charles M. Atkinson, general editor

Vol.	Composer: Title
1	Johannes Martini: *Secular Pieces*
2–8	*The Montpellier Codex. Parts I–IV*
9–10	Johannes Vincenet: *The Collected Works*
11–13	*The Conductus Collections of MS Wolfenbüttel 1099. Parts I–III*
14	*Fors seulement: Thirty Compositions for Three and Five Voices or Instruments from the Fifteenth and Sixteenth Centuries*
15	Johannes Cornago: *Complete Works*
16–18	*Beneventanum Troporum Corpus I. Tropes of the Proper of the Mass from Southern Italy,* A.D. *1000–1250*
19–26	*Beneventanum Troporum Corpus II. Ordinary Chants and Tropes for the Mass from Southern Italy,* A.D. *1000–1250. Parts 1–3*
27	*Beneventanum Troporum Corpus II. Ordinary Chants and Tropes for the Mass from Southern Italy,* A.D. *1000–1250. Part 4* [Not yet published]
28	*Beneventanum Troporum Corpus III. Indexes, Inventories, and Analytical Studies* [Not yet published]
29	*The Florence Laudario: An Edition of Florence, Biblioteca Nazionale Centrale, Banco Rari 18*
30–33	*Early Medieval Chants from Nonantola. Parts I–IV*
34–35	Johannes Martini: *Masses. Parts 1–2*
36	*De tous biens plaine: Twenty-Eight Settings of Hayne van Ghizeghem's Chanson*
37	*Fortuna desperata: Thirty-Six Settings of an Italian Song*
38	*Monophonic Tropes and Conductus of W1*
39–40	Johannes Martini and Johannes Brebis: *Sacred Music. Parts 1–2*